One Money, Many Countries

Monitoring the European Central Bank 2

Centre for Economic Policy Research

The Centre for Economic Policy Research is a network of almost 500 Research Fellows and Affiliates, based primarily in European universities. The Centre coordinates the research activities of its Fellows and Affiliates and communicates the results to the public and private sectors. CEPR is an entrepreneur, developing research initiatives with the producers, consumers and sponsors of research. Established in 1983, CEPR is a European economics research organization with uniquely wide-ranging scope and activities.

CEPR is a registered educational charity. Institutional (core) finance for the Centre is provided by major grants from the Economic and Social Research Council, under which an ESRC Resource Centre operates within CEPR; the Esmée Fairbairn Charitable Trust and the Bank of England. The Centre is also supported by the European Central Bank; the Bank for International Settlements; 22 national central banks and 45 companies. None of these organizations gives prior review to the Centre's publications, nor do they necessarily endorse the views expressed therein.

The Centre is pluralist and non-partisan, bringing economic research to bear on the analysis of medium- and long-run policy questions. CEPR research may include views on policy, but the Executive Committee of the Centre does not give prior review to its publications, and the Centre takes no institutional policy positions. The opinions expressed in this report are those of the authors and not those of the Centre for Economic Policy Research.

January 2000

Centre for Economic Policy Research
90-98 Goswell Road
London EC1V 7RR
UK
Tel: (44 20) 7878 2900   Fax: (44 20) 7878 2999
Email: cepr@cepr.org   Website: http://www.cepr.org

One Money, Many Countries

Monitoring the European Central Bank 2

Carlo Favero
IGIER, Università Bocconi, Milano, and CEPR

Xavier Freixas
Universidad Pompeu Fabra, Barcelona, and CEPR

Torsten Persson
Institute for International Economic Studies, Stockholm, and CEPR

Charles Wyplosz
The Graduate Institute of International Studies, Geneva, and CEPR

A member of citigroup.

MONTE
DEI PASCHI
DI SIENA
BANK SINCE 1472

The research underlying this publication was supported by Citibank, a member of Citigroup, and Monte dei Paschi di Siena S.p.A. The opinions expressed in this report are, however, those of the authors. Neither CEPR, Citibank nor Monte dei Paschi di Siena take any institutional policy positions.

Centre for Economic Policy Research
90-98 Goswell Road
London EC1V 7RR
UK

Tel: (44 20) 7878 2900
Fax: (44 20) 7878 2999
Email: cepr@cepr.org

Website: http://www.cepr.org

British Library Cataloguing in Publication Data
A catalogue record for this book is available from the British Library

ISBN: 1 898128 43 X

Printed and bound in the UK by Information Press, Oxford

Contents

MECB Statement of Purpose

Europe has a new central bank. It must develop its version of accountability and public debate over monetary policies. It is natural for CEPR, as a network of policy-oriented academic economists, to contribute to the establishment of a new tradition. Monitoring the European Central Bank (MECB), brings together a group of economists internationally known for their work on macroeconomics and monetary policy. MECB will monitor the European economy and the work of the ECB. Its analyses will be presented to the broader public, including the European Parliament and the media. A full MECB report is published each year complemented by a spring update that draws on recent publications of the ECB.

MECB acknowledges the financial support of Citibank, a member of Citigroup, and Monte dei Paschi di Siena S.p.A

MECB Steering Committee Members

David Begg, Birkbeck College, London, and CEPR

Paul De Grauwe, Katholieke Universiteit Leuven and CEPR

Pier Luigi Fabrizi, Monte dei Paschi di Siena S.p.A.

Francesco Giavazzi, Università Bocconi, Milano, and CEPR

Thomas Huertas, Citibank, A.G.

Richard Portes, London Business School and CEPR

Harald Uhlig, CentER, Tilburg University and CEPR

Charles Wyplosz, Graduate Institute of International Studies, Geneva, and CEPR

List of Figures

List of Tables

List of Boxes

Foreword

Just as the European Central Bank has quickly and fully established its authority in monetary policy-making, so the CEPR *Monitoring the European Central Bank* team has established its leadership among 'ECB-watchers'. Their analyses have been thoughtful and relevant, based on solid research but not 'academic' – indeed, occasionally rather provocative on the major policy issues facing the Bank. Their perspective has been pan-European, also following the model that the ECB has set out for itself. This is what CEPR intended, and we also believed from the beginning that it would be helpful to rotate membership of the group. So there are new participants in *MECB 2*, with some holdovers to provide continuity and consistency. We expect this pattern to continue.

The new report offers a review of the successful first year of the ECB and then focuses on two key issues: transparency, accountability, political legitimacy; and financial sector stability. In both areas, the report finds the current position unsatisfactory and it offers specific proposals for policy-makers (both inside and outside the Bank) to consider.

As for all CEPR publications, the views expressed here are those of the authors writing in their personal capacity. Their independence from CEPR and from the funders, Citigroup and Monte dei Paschi di Siena S.p.A., is at least as great as that of the ECB itself!

Thanks go to the CEPR staff members whose hard work and professionalism have ensured the successful execution of this project, and in particular to CEPR's Publications Manager, Sue Chapman, as well as to Linda Machin. The authors would particularly like to express their thanks to Giovanni Favara for research assistance; to Christina Lönnblad for editorial assistance; and to Axel Weber for providing hospitality at the Centre for Financial Studies in Frankfurt.

RICHARD PORTES
24 January 2000

Executive Summary

The year in review

- In a relatively calm environment, the ECB had a successful first year and displayed more flexibility than expected regarding asymmetries within the euro-zone.

- Tender auctions through which the ECB provides banks with liquidity have remained heavily oversubscribed throughout the year. This leads to inefficiencies in the allocation of liquidity. Moving from fixed rates with rationing to flexible, market-clearing rates would solve the difficulty without reducing ECB control.

- TARGET, the wholesale payment system set up by the ECB, has delivered on its promises and has successfully linked up with other pan-European wholesale systems. Retail payments, however, remain far too costly due to antiquated and anti-competitive practices.

- The ECB's policy strategy remains difficult to interpret. The monetary policy framework, with its emphasis on 'two pillars', seems better designed to conceal strategy than to help the public understand it. Not only do the words fail to reveal the ECB's reasoning, but they do not always match its deeds.

- European long-term interest rates continue to be heavily influenced by conditions in the US. Along with the behaviour of the euro vs. the dollar, this suggests that market participants are not yet fully convinced that the ECB will treat the euro–dollar exchange rate with benign neglect.

Transparency and accountability

■ The ECB has been seen as lacking transparency and accountability, especially when compared with the Bank of England. These central banks differ in one key aspect: the ECB is goal-independent – it decides what price stability means in practice without any political counterweight – whereas the Bank of England is goal-dependent – the Chancellor of the Exchequer sets its inflation target. This difference shows up in various institutional and operational features:

  □ *Political responsibility:* the ECB Governing Council arbitrates among conflicting short-run interests, whereas the Bank of England's Monetary Policy Committee (MPC) fulfils a technical task.

  □ *Transparency about policy:* the ECB is *ex post* transparent, to be judged on whether it has achieved its stated goals; the Bank of England is *ex ante* transparent, it explains how it intends to meet its assigned goals.

  □ *Accountability for decisions:* the ECB Council makes decisions on the basis of collective accountability, the Bank of England's MPC members are individually accountable.

  □ *Appointments:* ECB Executive Board members are appointed for eight-year single terms, MPC members are appointed for three-year renewable terms.

  □ *Reputations:* the ECB aims at gradually achieving a collective reputation as a goal-setting institution, MPC members build individual reputations by achieving goals set elsewhere.

■ The ECB's ultimate challenge is to gain political legitimacy. Here it suffers from two handicaps:

  □ as a goal-setting institution its actions are open to political debate.

  □ the chains of delegation and control from citizens to the Governing Council are long and complex, with no possibility of issuing instructions.

■ Moreover, the ECB's design is adapted to national interests (a feature it shares with other EU institutions such as the Commission). National conflicts are probably not the most relevant ones in the short-run design of European monetary policy. Other relevant coalitions of interests (e.g. creditors vs. debtors, insiders vs. outsiders in labour markets) that cross national borders find no representation.

Financial sector stability

- Systemic risk in banking and financial markets might increase or decline with EMU, as forces operate in both directions. Without appropriate supervision, regulation and institution-building, the risk-enhancing forces will prevail.

- Growing interbank transactions create a web of exposures capable of transmitting financial failures across Europe in domino-like fashion.

- Current arrangements make national taxpayers bear the costs of bank bailouts, which provides appropriate incentives for regulation and supervision remaining at the national level. Still, two difficulties emerge:

  - Emergency interventions involve not only the supply of liquidity, which the ECB is well equipped to provide. They also require real-time coordination of targeted private lending to keep troubled institutions operating, which can become a problem given the dispersion of decision-making authority and information.

  - The creation of trans-national financial institutions raises new questions about who ultimately bears the costs of emergency support.

Proposals

- Institutional reform. The coming inter-governmental conference (IGC) has the explicit task of preparing the EU for enlargement. We offer the following proposals:

  - Reduce national influence in the ECB's Governing Council in favour of the Executive Board. This could be achieved by introducing revolving terms for national central bank (NCB) governors according to a pre-set schedule. The size of the Council should stay fixed as new countries join EMU.

  - Give the European Parliament a greater role in the appointment of the Executive Board. Simultaneous reform of the Parliament election rules should foster the building of cross-border coalitions and true European parties.

  - Remove the goal independence of the ECB and specialise its mission to the technical task of implementing a well-specified goal – in the form of an inflation target – set by the European Parliament (after appropriate electoral reform).

▮ Short-run measures to be taken by the ECB itself:

▢ We do not support proposals to publish individual voting records and minutes focusing on individual differences (until institutional reforms have made the ECB goal-dependent). The Governing Council can build a collective reputation.

▢ Shift to *ex ante* transparency about policy by publishing the ESCB's internal forecasts and by presenting alternative contingency policy plans.

▮ Financial stability. The ECB's ability to cope with systemic crises is untested so far. Three possible solutions can be envisaged:

▢ *Status quo.* The SCB develops procedures to deal swiftly with possibly contagious bank failures.

▢ *Centralised.* An independent European regulatory body is set up as a counterpart to the ECB to take over functions currently exercised at the national level.

▢ *Decentralised.* Markets are allowed to perform more monitoring and evaluating functions, based on Europe-wide disclosure principles, supplemented with incentives designed to enhance financial soundness and mechanisms for prompt corrective action and orderly closure of failing financial institutions. The ECB can use its constitutional rights to issue or initiate legislation to get this process going.

The status quo is risky. The centralised solution is not politically viable in the near future because it requires relinquishing national control and a Treaty revision, even if this is the way to go in the long run. Decentralisation becomes the relevant interim solution, with the ECB in charge of avoiding systemic events triggered by illiquidity and each national Treasury in charge of avoiding that large institutions trigger systemic crises.

1

The year in review

The year 1999 started with concerns about the crises in Southeast Asia, Russia and Brazil. It ended with the ECB's first interest rate hike, while the euro continued to depreciate against the US dollar and the yen. All in all, the first year of the euro has turned out to be quite smooth. The world environment has mostly been subdued, the main disturbance being the rise in oil prices. The ECB has been able to concentrate mostly on domestic issues, an ideal situation for its maiden flight.

So far, the economic record is quite encouraging. Reactions to the two interest-rate cuts (in December 1998 and April 1999) were highly positive, helping the ECB to establish its credibility not just as an inflation-fighter but also as a well-rounded central bank willing to take on board broader concerns. The November decision to raise the interest rate was also well received, serving as an indication that the ECB remains vigilant on the inflation front. At the same time, the ECB's communication strategy remains controversial and its position on bank supervision needs clarification.

Issues concerning monetary stability – including communication, accountability, and transparency – are examined more closely in Chapter 2 of this report. Financial stability – including supervision, and the prevention and management of systemic crises – is the main subject of Chapter 3. Chapter 4 brings together our conclusions and recommendations. This first chapter takes a closer look at the year, while introducing some of the later topics.

1.1 General economic situation

Inflation

Inflation remained in the lower part of the 0–2% target range until mid-year. Early in the year, there were even concerns about deflation, partly erased in April by the ECB's decision to lower its intervention rate. Since the summer, inflation has been rising by

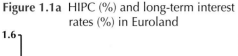

Figure 1.1a HIPC (%) and long-term interest rates (%) in Euroland

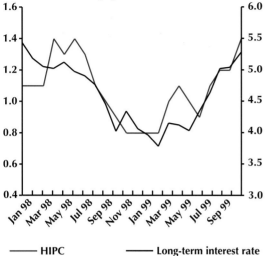

HIPC (left-hand scale) — Long-term interest rate (right-hand scale)

Figure 1.1b A measure of expected inflation in Euroland (long *minus* short term interst rates) (%)

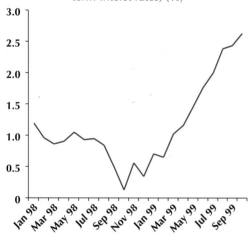

Source: Datastream

Figure 1.2 European inflation (%)

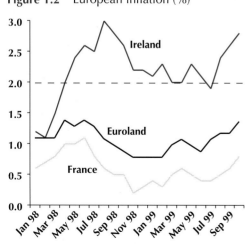

Source: Datastream

about 0.5 percentage points – a small increase that the ECB attributes mostly to oil price rises. By October, the ECB started to send signals that it was concerned by the increase in inflation; thus by November a hike in the interest rate hardly came as a surprise. The interaction between inflation and interest rates raises two issues: the room for manoeuvre the ECB leaves for itself and the variability of inflation rates throughout the euro zone.

As lags between policy decisions and the maximum impact on inflation are known to exceed one year, the ECB needs to act preventively well ahead. The 0–2% target range implies little room for manoeuvre in situations when expectations react strongly to the current inflation rate. Figure 1.1 indicates that this was indeed the case in 1999: the long-term interest rate moved quite closely with the inflation rate.

This co-movement could reflect a rise either in inflationary expectations or in the real interest rate. Figure 1.1b shows one measure of expected inflation – the difference between long- and short-term interest rates – turning around quite quickly early in the year, and trending upward since the second quarter. (As we shall see in Chapter 2 other measures of expected inflation display a similar pattern.) Seen in this light, the April interest rate cut reflected less concern about deflation *per se* – as many commentators argued – than doubts about resuming growth in two of Euroland's largest countries, Germany and Italy.

The second issue concerns the dispersion of inflation rates throughout the euro zone. Figure 1.2. shows the zone to be far from homogeneous in that respect. The ECB's stated intention is to concentrate on the average rate, and that is the right approach. Inflation rates diverge for two main reasons: different trends and cyclical positions.

Trends are likely to differ across the zone. Price and wage levels are notoriously lower in poorer areas. As the less advanced areas are likely to catch up, however, their prices and wages will gradually approach those in the currently most advanced economies, leading to higher trend inflation. Those trends reflect structural, non-monetary forces and should have no bearing on the ECB's actions except for one issue. As the HIPC is an average of national rates, in steering the HIPC inflation rate the ECB also determines the trend rates of individual countries. In particular, a lower rate of HIPC inflation implies lower trend inflation in the most advanced countries. Since inflation in each country is in itself the average of diverse positions across industries, a very low rate may require declining prices and wages in some industries (This is an application of an argument originally made by Akerlof et al.(1996)). With a floor for nominal wage increases at zero, an ambitious ECB target may generate serious tensions. The more diverse is the euro zone, the larger will be the dispersion of national inflation rates and the more acute the corresponding problem for the most advanced industries in the most advanced countries.

Cyclical positions will always vary to some extent across the zone, an issue that has been at centre of the EMU debate. Shocks can be asymmetric and even symmetric shocks need not have exactly the same effects in every country. In addition, fiscal policy agendas might differ across nations. Some countries will therefore occasionally experience booms with inflation significantly above the Euroland average, as has been the case in 1999 in Ireland and Spain (See Figures 1.3a and 1.3b). The reason for concern is not these divergences *per se* but the effect of local cycles.

The generic problem is known as *the Walters critique*. As Box 1.1 explains, runaway inflation or deflation are ruled out. But as the ECB is not expected to stabilize local cycles, these could well become wider than in the past. Perhaps more importantly, a period of above-average inflation leaves a country with reduced competitiveness, and must be followed by a period of below-average inflation to recapture the lost ground. Downward rigidities for prices and wages can make such cycles painful and protracted. In addition, local cycles may also translate into asset price booms and busts, especially in markets for commercial and private property. These might further amplify local fluctuations and, possibly, also threaten financial stability, as asset market volatility sometimes goes hand in hand with serious financial turbulence.

The response will partly take the form of market adjustments. Individual investors and financial institutions will learn to hedge more volatile local asset prices, partly through asset and liability diversification, partly through more prudent investments. Yet, experience suggests that private markets often fail to react smoothly and swiftly, which means that the ECB might not be able to turn a blind eye to national divergences. We return to this question in Chapter 3.

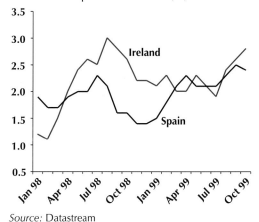

Figure 1.3a CPI (harmonized) inflation in Spain and Ireland (%)

Source: Datastream

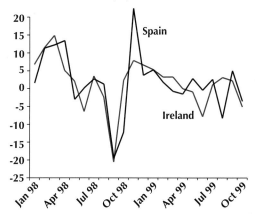

Figure 1.3b Asset price growth in Spain and Ireland (%)

Source: Datastream

BOX 1.1 The Walters critique

A long time ago, Alan Walters – Margaret Thatcher's economic adviser – observed that monetary policy in a monetary union might be destabilizing. With a common nominal interest rate, the real interest rate is lower where the inflation rate is higher. To the extent that monetary policy operates through the real interest rate, it will be more expansionary where inflation and growth are higher, and less expansionary where growth and inflation are low.

Could this trigger endless spirals of inflation or deflation? Only in a world where monetary policy operates solely through the interest rate. But monetary policy also operates through external competitiveness (the real exchange rate), asset prices and available credit. As higher inflation means less competitiveness, it eventually hurts asset prices and reduces the purchasing power of credit, these channels are stabilizing. In practice, existing monetary unions, such as the US or European countries which bring together disparate regions, do not seem to suffer from the Walters critique (See Figure B1.1).

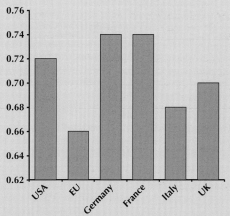

Figure B1.1 Business cycle correlations

Source: Fatas (1998)

Note: Business cycles are measured as GDP growth in the US and EU, and as regional employment growth in Germany, France, Italy and the UK.

Table 1.1 GDP growth and unemployment in Euroland

	Unemployment rate (%)		GDP growth rate (%)		
	98	99*	98	99 Q1**	99 Q2**
Austria	4.7	4.3	3.3	1.2	1.7
Belgium	9.5	9.0	2.9	1.7	1.7
Finland	11.4	10.0	5.6	3.4	3.3
France	11.7	11.0	3.4	2.4	2.1
Germany	9.4	9.1	2.0	0.6	0.6
Ireland	7.8	6.7	8.9		
Italy	11.9	11.4	1.3	0.8	0.8
Netherlands	4.0	3.2	3.2	3.1	3.1
Spain	18.8	15.6	4.0	3.2	3.6
Portugal	5.1	4.8	3.5		

Source: Eurostat
* Latest montly data available
** annualized % change

Figure 1.4 Dispersion of shocks to national GDP growth 1963–99 (%)

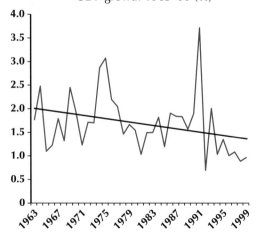

Growth and unemployment

Table 1.1 reports GDP growth and unemployment rates in the Euroland-11 countries over the last two years. Clearly, this period is characterized by different conditions throughout the area, even if one takes structural differences into account. Most European countries experienced a recession in the early 1990s, slow growth during the Maastricht convergence years and were resuming a better performance when the emerging markets crisis hit in 1997. While this could have been an instance of a rather small symmetric crisis, the effects seem asymmetric. Trade composition is one possible reason; another is the ability of countries to face moderate shocks.

This divergence has challenged the ECB's determination to limit its attention to Europe-wide averages. That France, Germany and Italy were all growing slowly could not be ignored in early 1999, especially as these three countries faced budget deficits close to the limit set by the Stability Pact. The ECB's April decision to reduce interest rates was quite appropriate but – as further discussed below – not well explained. The ECB's reluctance to acknowledge any concern for growth and unemployment is part of the problem, but another is precisely the existence of divergences across countries. The latter thus emerges as EMU's Achilles heel.

One view on the cyclical effects of EMU is that the single currency will deepen integration and make business cycles in the zone more coherent. Another is that EMU will exacerbate divergences, as the Stability and Growth Pact will prevent national fiscal policy from replacing national monetary policy as a tool of stabilization. Both views may hold some truth. Europe's experience in the last three decades gives limited support to the first, integrationist view. Figure 1.4 displays the average of standard deviation of shocks to national GDP growth rates across the EU-15 countries from 1963 to 1999. The trend line shows a decline in cyclical divergence across the European countries, but it is only marginally statistically significant (t = 1.67).

Does the early experience of EMU help clarify the relevance of the second, divergence view? Chapter 2 sheds some light on this question: counterfactual experiments suggest that the ECB has in fact smoothed divergence out. By the year's end, there are clear indications that growth is picking up in the large laggard countries.

Exchange rate

The dollar appreciation during 1999 has clearly complicated things for the ECB. It has been widely interpreted as a euro depreciation, raising questions about the strength of the currency. The upper chart in Figure 1.5 compares the euro and the Swiss franc exchange rates *vis-à-vis* the dollar. The euro has been weaker than the Swiss franc from late 1998 onwards, but only slightly so, and yet no one has seen the franc as weak currency. Importantly, we must keep in mind that such bilateral exchange rates are relative measures, using a particular currency – here the dollar – as a yardstick. The yardstick, however, is not appropriate when it is fluctuating. Moreover, with the birth of a new major currency, the euro, it is less plausible than before to treat the dollar as a natural yardstick.

This is why the lower chart in Figure 1.5 presents a wider definition, the effective exchange rate computed as a trade-weighted average of a currency's exchange rate *vis-à-vis* a basket of currencies. In comparison with the two other major currencies, the dollar and the yen, the euro appears to have been more stable over the period 1998–9, peaking in late 1998 and then returning slightly below its value of early 1998. While the yen has increased considerably – in fact recovering from a clearly undervalued level in 1998, there is little difference in the behaviour of the euro and the dollar. Lamenting a weak euro is patently unjustified.

More precisely, over 1999 we see a dollar appreciation early in the year (the dollar strengthening vs. both the euro and the yen), then a strong yen appreciation (the yen strengthening vs. both the dollar and the euro). Good news about the US economy explains the first period, indications that Japan is finally growing after years of misery explain the latter. In this interpretation, movements of the euro effective exchange rate to a large extent reflected events taking place in the two other large economies. Part of the weakening, however, might reflect the news that Italy and Germany were slow to resume growth. Such weakness would be a normal and welcome market reaction, helping export growth in these countries.

Inevitably, some observers voiced the complaint that the euro is not 'as strong as the mark'. This is wrong, of course. The strength of a currency can only be assesd in the long run, and the Deutsche mark itself has experienced numerous episodes of appreciation followed by depreciation, normal events under floating exchange rates. Yet, calls on the ECB to clarify its position on the exchange rate reflect the public's eagerness to decipher early signals of the long run orientation of monetary policy, as well as some ambiguity in the bank's strategy. For most of the year the ECB has publicly expressed confidence in the long-run outlook for the currency, which has raised the spectre of benign neglect. Facing increasing nervousness toward the end of the year, the ECB explicitly rejected benign neglect, prompting rumours of pending foreign exchange market interventions. This is one of several examples where the ECB has communicated its intentions in an ambiguous way; in this case the ambiguity may have been intentional. It was certainly surprising that the ECB would explicitly link the euro's weakness to the German government's bailout of a construction company in December. Such a statement opens up a public conflict with a major government on a minor

Figure 1.5   Exchange rates in 1998–9

Exchange rates *vis-à-vis* the US dollar (weekly data)

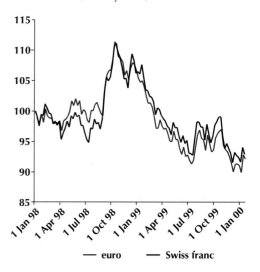

Effective exchange rates (weekly data)

Source: Datastream

policy issue. But it also reflects a concern with the euro's value and further deepens the mystery of the two-pillar strategy.

1.2 The two-pillar strategy

The ECB has announced that its strategy rests on one goal and two pillars. The goal is price stability defined as HIPC inflation between 0 and 2%. One pillar is a money growth reference target, the other comprises a number of unspecified indicators including the exchange rate and asset prices. At a time when more and more central banks replace money-growth targeting with (expected) inflation targeting, and make efforts at being transparent, the ECB's strategy is unavoidably seen as obscure, often even archaic. Two main issues emerge from the debate:[1]

- How broad should the framework be?

- How transparent should the central bank be; in particular, how closely should its words and deeds correspond?

Targets

Monetary targets were in vogue in the 1980s, following the examples set by the Bundesbank and the Federal Reserve. Such targets played a key role in successfully bringing down inflation from the high rates following the oil shocks. Once inflation had settled down, the instrument gradually appeared too blunt, because the link between money growth and inflation is too imprecise. In addition, the combination of low inflation and financial deregulation has deeply changed the menu of financial instruments, further eroding the stability of monetary aggregates. Following New Zealand, many central banks adopted inflation targets in the 1990s (e.g. Canada, the UK, Sweden, Australia, Spain, Israel, and Japan).[2] Two important exceptions remained the Bundesbank and the Federal Reserve.

The Fed has adopted a pragmatic policy strategy, stressing its commitment to low inflation and steady growth. It reacts to a wide range of indicators, sharing its reasoning with the public in its statements and releasing minutes of the policy-making Open Market Committee after 6 weeks. Until the end of last year the Bundesbank retained its money growth targets, restating its commitment to price stability and keeping its deliberations confidential.

The ECB has largely adopted the Bundesbank's prior approach, making somewhat more precise its definition of price stability. In the description of its strategy, the ECB notes that the two

---

1. The exchange between Buiter (1999) and Issing (1999) encapsulates this debate.
2. Bernanke et al. (1999) describe and discuss the experience with inflation targeting, both in general and in specific countries.

pillars are not exact yardsticks, but devices used by the Board to analyse the economic situation and conduct its deliberations. Critics of the ECB complain about continuing adherence to an older framework and a notable lack of transparency.

Transparency and accountability

Critics observe that the multiplication of targets and indicators make it difficult to understand how the ECB reaches its decisions, thus reducing its transparency and accountability. Transparency is deemed important because surprises unsettle financial markets while uncertainty might result in higher borrowing costs. Accountability is seen as the necessary counterpart to independence, bringing appointed officials under the scrutiny of the broad public that they serve. As one of the most independent central banks in the world, the critics argue, the ECB has to be highly transparent and strictly accountable.

The ECB indeed considers itself to be transparent and accountable. Its Board members insist (see Issing, 1999) that they fully report the tenor of their deliberations and thoroughly explain their decisions. They add that price stability, the mandate set by the Maastricht Treaty, is the yardstick by which they will be judged, and they note that their definition of price stability is both precise and fully verifiable.

The critics (e.g. Svensson, 1999), on the other hand, argue that an inflation target as specified by the ECB is not verifiable. Inflation is not entirely controllable by a central bank, because both shocks – such as fluctuations in energy prices or exchange rates, changes in investment behaviour, and financial turbulence – and policy affect inflation in ways impossible to interpret with sufficient precision. Outcomes at variance with the stated target may thus always be explained away by the central bank. True accountability, the critics claim, requires the central bank to routinely publish its own forecasts regarding inflation, explicitly taking account of shocks as they occur to explain deviations of the expected inflation rate from the target. Inflation forecasts, they say, constitute a precise and relevant intermediate target allowing the central bank to communicate its interpretation of how changes in the indicators it monitors affect the ultimate target, inflation.

So far the ECB has refused to publish its forecasts of inflation (and output). It argues that forecasts are too inaccurate to become the sole indicator of its analysis, especially in the early years of the euro when financial markets adjust and, more generally, when the broad public learns how to operate in a radically new environment. The ECB claims to act like the US Fed, keeping an open mind and making the best use of many indicators.

Critics also complain that the ECB does not provide *bona fide* accounts of its deliberations (e.g. Buiter, 1999a). Voting records, they maintain, provide useful information on how Board members identify and deal with the main points of contention inherent in monetary policy making.[3] Apparently, the ECB Governing Council does not always vote, but reaches its decisions by consensus (President Duisenberg, press conference 7 October 1999).

The mode of decision making thus emerges as an important issue. To the ECB, consensus may appear the proper way to proceed for several reasons. It encourages agreement and discourages polarisation, which is deemed important in the European context where the ECB serves many different public opinions, with the risk of disagreements boiling over into national conflicts. Consensus also operates as a learning device for Board members who come from different traditions, with the risk of serious misunderstanding.

In all fairness, many roads lead to Rome: transparency and accountability have different meanings in different societies, ranging from a tradition of full openness in the Nordic countries, over a Germanic respect for authority, to a culture of ambiguity in the Mediterranean fringes of Europe. While some traditions may serve the public interest better than others, we must acknowledge that traditions cannot be changed overnight. Europe cannot be built in one day. What matters, ultimately, is that the broad public has sufficient understanding of the ECB's actions to pass judgement. This raises the issue of how the ECB communicates.

ECB's public relations: words vs. deeds

The ECB has promptly developed several channels of communication: it publishes a *Monthly Bulletin*, it operates a fairly elaborate website, and Council meetings are immediately followed by a press conference attended by the President and the Vice President. Communication is therefore at a high frequency, especially if one adds the various speeches by Board members (available at the website) that appear to be closely coordinated. The *Bulletin* is of generally high quality, as is the website.[4] Yet the press conferences give an irritating impression of being designed to carefully doctor the information released to the public, with an eye to making the ECB look good but not transparent.

In fact, the public relations strategy of the ECB is closely related to the monetary policy framework. It rests on repetitive and uninformative restatements – for instance, that monetary policy is 'stability-oriented', that there are 'two equally important pillars and many indicators' – without engaging the debates reported above. Every central bank observer knows that

---

3. The publications of minutes is also a source of controversy. It must be noted that minutes are always edited and that, when they are published, serious negotiations can take place outside of the Boardroom.
4. For an appraisal of the *Monthly Bulletin*, see Tabellini (1999).

monetary policy cannot simultaneously pursue several objectives. The ECB has adopted a strategy that is impossible to carry out, if taken literally.

Reasonably, the framework has not been taken literally: the money targets have been overrun (see Table 1.2), the euro has been allowed to depreciate and local conditions in the largest countries have weighed on the decision to lower the interest rate. Yet, public pronouncements accompanying these decisions have often claimed the contrary. Occasional gaffes are unavoidable, especially at an early stage, but the repeated words contradicting deeds appears far too systematic to be random errors. Some examples from the first year illustrate the problem and the associated risks.

▪ The interest rate cut of April 8 was clearly an (appropriate) response to a deterioration of the situation in Germany and Italy. The President's statement carefully refrained from confronting the asymmetry of the situation:

In the euro area, overall growth prospects worsened towards the end of last year, as reported when we met in early March. In the meantime, official data confirm that real GDP growth in the euro area weakened in the fourth quarter of 1998, when compared with the previous quarter. The weakness is particularly apparent in the manufacturing sector, where confidence deteriorated further. Partial information covering a substantial part of the euro area appears to confirm this picture. Most recent data on total employment in the euro area point to a certain deceleration in net job creation in the last quarter of 1998.

(Duisenberg, press conference, April 8, 1999)

Sticking to a minimalist interpretation of its own actions, the ECB revealed an inclination for obfuscation, in contrast to its commitment to transparency, which casts a shadow on how much trust can be put in its words.

▪ Achievement of the monetary target does not particularly concern the public and most ECB watchers. In attempting to explain the overruns, the ECB clearly intends to signal its commitment to the monetary pillar. Thereby it is led to provide detailed explanations, which appear unconvincing as they rely on a relationship which seems to have become highly unreliable. At the same time, overruns of the 1999 reference value lead to seemingly contradictory statements:

The reference value for monetary growth is an important part of the first pillar of the strategy, which assigns a prominent role to the analysis of monetary developments. [...] The reference value therefore does not entail a commitment on the part of the Eurosystem to correct mechanistically deviations of monetary growth from the reference value.

(Review of the quantitative reference value for monetary growth, ECB, press release, 2 December 1999)

▪ The depreciation of the euro has been seen as auspicious by many observers. The ECB's initial response has been to

Table 1.2   M3 in euro area in 1999
(annual percentage change)

	M3	3-month MA	Ref. value
Jan	5.7	5.1	4.5
Feb	5.1	5.4	4.5
Mar	5.5	5.3	4.5
Apr	5.3	5.4	4.5
May	5.4	5.4	4.5
June	5.4	5.6	4.5
July	5.9	5.7	4.5
Aug	5.8	6.0	4.5
Sep	6.2	6.0	4.5
Oct	6.0		4.5

Source: ECB

affirm a policy of benign neglect, an apparent contradiction of earlier statements that the euro will be as good as the mark. As noted above, however, there is no contradiction. The refusal to deal openly with the issue has fuelled further depreciation on the mistaken view that the ECB does not have the resolve to make the euro a strong currency. All in all, the general impression is that the Executive Board and the Governing Council have not formed a view on one of the most important roles of the bank, or worse that disagreements exist amongst their members.

In all three instances, the actions were right at the time they were taken. The ECB could have explained its reasoning and shared its doubts without endangering its leadership in any way. 'Say what you do' is clearly a lesson that the ECB should learn from its first year's experience.

The apparent contradiction between words and deeds is further explored in Chapter 2. Using the information gleaned from the 1999 experience, we attempt to reveal the logic behind the deeds and interpret the logic behind the words. Overall, we recognise the tradition of 'Euro-fudge', the contradiction between two logics underpinning European integration for several decades: the will to go for far-reaching, efficient economic integration and the desire to retain power at the national level.

1.3 | Financial markets

The financial environment in Europe is changing. We have witnessed multiple domestic mergers in the European banking industry. Signs are apparent of far-reaching disintermediation under way. Important changes have occurred in the way the financial markets operate and settle transactions. Some of these changes affect the ECB's tasks only indirectly as they might affect financial stability. Two other aspects, however, touch directly on the ECB's responsibility: the creation and channelling of liquidity, and cross-border payment systems.

The supply of liquidity

Nowadays central banks inject liquidity in pretty much the same way in every developed country: pre-scheduled repo auctions provide the bulk of the banking system's liquidity, while marginal lending and deposit facilities allow banks to cope with exceptional liquidity shocks in the period between two auctions. Still, these auctions are organized in different ways, which can have significant allocation effects. We can distinguish the following three classes of auctions:

- In a *flexible-rate* tender, the supply of liquidity is always equal to demand above the marginal rate. The actual final allocation may be based on the bid rate of each institution or on the marginal rate, or on some combination of the two, but these differences are minor.

- In a *fixed-rate* tender with *variable quantities,* the supply of liquidity is determined by demand at a pre-announced fixed rate.

- In a *fixed-rate* tender with *fixed quantities,* neither price nor quantity is market clearing; through a rationing scheme, each bidding institution gets an amount of liquidity in proportion to its initial bid.

Among the EMU countries Austria, Ireland, Italy, Portugal and Spain, used flexible-rate tenders, whereas Finland, France, Germany and the Netherlands practised fixed-rate tenders. The ECB has decided to combine a fixed-rate/fixed-quantity tender on a weekly basis with a flexible-rate tender on a monthly basis. The argument in favour of the fixed-rate/fixed-quantity choice is twofold: the ECB's reputation is enhanced by adopting the Bundesbank's former procedure, and it sends strong signals to the market regarding both the interest rate and the monetary objective. This procedure has the drawback, however, of simply ignoring the financial markets.

The overbidding problem

In its weekly repo auctions the ECB offers liquidity for two weeks against collateral. Banks bid for a share of liquidity at the pre-announced rate. If the total of the received bids exceed the supply of liquidity that the ECB wishes to supply, each bank may be rationed down to an allotment proportional to its bid. Depending on the amount of liquidity demanded, the ECB may either change the total amount of liquidity provided, or simply adjust the ratio of allotment to demand. The wide swings in the allotment ratio documented in Figure 1.6 indicate that the latter course has been chosen: ratios range from 0.06 to 0.33 reaching 1 on just one occasion.

The rationing has been more severe than that in Germany before EMU, with an average ECB allotment ratio half that of the Bundesbank. It is difficult to establish whether this reflects European banks bidding more aggressively or the ECB holding more aggressively to a monetary target. What is clear is that wide swings in allotment ratios may be associated with costs.

Indeed, in the countries which previously operated flexible rate tenders the ECB has been heavily criticized for strangling liquidity. In a way the criticism is unfair, since adopting a common mechanism for liquidity provision must unavoidably impose the costs of learning the new rules of the game on some countries. Complaints are the price of convergence and are not to be taken seriously, except if financial institutions accustomed to an efficient environment are forced to adapt to an inefficient

Figure 1.6   Allotment ratio and the fixed rate tender interest rate (%)

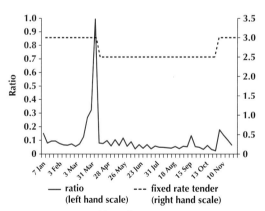

Source: ECB *Monthly Bulletin*

one. It would be an oversimplification, however, to attribute overbidding problems entirely to initial learning. It is true that some banks did not overbid or were cautious to overbid if they lacked collateral in the first months of EMU. It is also true that subsidiary cross-border credit lines, allowing a bank from a liquidity-short country to borrow from a bank in a country with excess liquidity, were not in place. But banks have now adapted and the overbidding problem remains.

In our view the overbidding problem has been exaggerated. Banks can draw on their reserves to cope with liquidity shocks since the reserve requirement has to be respected only as a monthly average. Also, the monthly repo auctions (with two months maturity) are operated as flexible rate tenders, which allow banks to obtain necessary liquidity at the market rate.

Still, there is a qualitative difference whether the allotment ratio is 80% or 10%. At 80%, rationing is marginal and the interest rate adequately signals the ECB target. At 10%, the rate bears no connection with the market, the incentives to overbid are exacerbated and there is excessive uncertainty such that banks may end up holding too much collateral. As the ECB weekly auction seems to fit the latter case, it is worth emphasising how this mechanism allocates liquidity.

- The combination of collateral and uncertainty limits the bids of participating banks. Banks confident in an allotment ratio of 10% would obtain exactly their required amount of liquidity and the allotment ratio would not matter. With the auction rate below the market rate, why do banks not bid even larger amounts, particularly as they need collateral only to cover the allotted amount?[5] The answer lies in the uncertainty about the allotment ratio: aggressive overbidding may yield excessive liquidity, which is costly, if market rates fall.

- The mechanism gives a very large premium to those assets constituting eligible collateral. This creates double uncertainty: the premium depends on the difference between the weekly auction fixed rate and the market rate and there is no guarantee that an asset eligible as collateral will not drop out of the list.

- As a consequence there was some discrimination – at least early in the year – in favour of those credit institutions whose bonds are eligible as collateral.[6] Banks in some

5. Initially it was unclear whether the institution had to provide an amount of collateral equal to the total amount of its bid or an amount equal to the liquidity it was alloted. The issue was settled at the begining of February: the collateral required was to be sufficient for backing only the alloted amount.

6. The composition of collateral at the end of March 1999 was: government paper represented 76%; credit institution paper 18%, with the residual 6% issued by the corporate sector and central banks (*ECB Bulletin*, May 1999)

countries, such as Spain, were lead to undertake a process of loan securitization, keeping the securities in their portfolio to use them in repo operations. There was also some discrimination in favour of those countries where banks had a larger fraction of eligible assets in their portfolios.

These negatives should not be exaggerated, though. Financial institutions buy and sell collateral. Banks that lack collateral must naturally bear the full discipline of unsecured borrowing and be subject to more careful peer monitoring in the interbank markets. This all improves the efficiency of the banking system.

Why then has the ECB not switched to flexible rate tenders to eliminate the undesirable features of fixed rate tenders with rationing? The ECB's main response is that a fixed rate signals the appropriate rate of interest. Yet, under rationing, it is the interbank market interest rate, not the tender rate, that reflects the true cost of liquidity. The market uses the marginal rates in the lending (as a ceiling) and deposit (as a floor) facilities as a stronger signal than the tender rate since these ECB facilities are open to banks with eligible collateral. It is not clear to us why the ECB sticks to an inefficient rule. If it is to develop a reputation of consistency in its decisions, is it worth sticking to a decision even when it is the wrong one?

Payments Systems

At its very early stages the European Monetary Institute realized that an integrated payment system would be the backbone of financial integration in Europe. This is why Article 3.1 of the Statute of the ESCB stipulates that it shall 'promote the smooth operation of payment systems'. The result, a fully collateralized trans-European payment system, TARGET, allows settlements of euro payments through accounts at any of the 15 national central banks of the European Union, and in certain cases at the ECB. In particular, euro-denominated payments can be made via a real-time gross settlement (RTGS) system, which accounts for the linking through TARGET of the bulk of large-volume transactions.

The general perception is that TARGET is a remarkable accomplishment, successfully implemented with only minor problems at the learning stage. Operators using TARGET have preferred to delay payments, sending them late in the day. In addition to the obvious preference of delaying payments until receiving other payments, these timing problems depend on a number of factors, including different closing hours in different markets.

Other private cross-border large-value payment systems have emerged as complements to TARGET. Fortunately, their systemic risk is limited because of adequate caps on bank positions. The main competitor to TARGET on cross-border payments is the European Banker's Association (EBA) system, but there is some specialization as TARGET is used mainly for large transactions. Although EBA processes twice as many payments, it accounts for only half of TARGET's value of cross-border transactions. Other payment systems, such as Euro Access Frankfurt or Paris Net Settlement, are competing on both the domestic and cross-border markets.

Initially, the co-existing channels for cross-border payments raised some difficulties, mainly because different banks tended to prefer different systems. A receiving bank did not know whether it would receive funds via TARGET, or through another channel. This has necessitated some coordination between paying and receiving banks, particularly in the first few months after the launch of TARGET. Mutual agreements have solved those problems. A formal swap mechanism between EBA and TARGET now copes with banks' liquidity imbalances between the two systems.

'Smooth operation of payment systems' concerns *retail* as well as wholesale operations. This is the dark side of the European payment system. So far, retail customers' expectations of diminished costs for cross-border payments have not been fulfilled. Despite the introduction of the euro, cross-border payments fees are substantially higher than their domestic equivalent. Moreover, the fees are more widely dispersed across financial institutions. Competition in the banking industry should progressively drive the fees down, but there are some countervailing forces.

- A major barrier to competition is the existence of contractual interbank relationships, known as correspondent banking. The pervasiveness of correspondent banking thwarts the pressure on banks to change their internal organization even though it entails higher costs, since higher costs are passed back to customers' fees.

- The ubiquity of correspondent banking has stalled the standardization of retail payments in electronic format, which would allow banks to route cross-border payments automatically and provide interfaces with the procedures for domestic payments. Even though a workable standard for cross-border payment, IBAN (International Bank Account Number), has been developed, it has not been implemented.

The Eurosystem has given full priority to the successful implementation of large-value payment systems. But it will have to tackle the issue of retail payments in the near future.

Market integration in EMU

Integration in the *money market* has been spectacular. The unsecured deposit market has been more completely integrated, however, than the repo market. Banks continue to hold as collateral securities in their own country to avoid the costs and inconvenience of cross-border collateral. The reason is the absence of reliable links (such as DvP) between national securities settlements systems. Costs could also be eliminated by consolidation of the national systems; European securities are now in 31 depositories,compared wtih 3 in the US. The problem does not seem technical but political, reflecting nationalistic concerns about local financial centres (IMF, 1999). It is regrettable that such protectionist tendencies are allowed to hamper the integration of the safer repo market.

Integration of *securities markets* has not been as fast, because of differences in market infrastructure, as well as in the legal, regulatory, and institutional regimes. In spite of this, bond-market integration has been remarkable. In the government debt market, governments have harmonized their issues, with all member countries switching to the same accounting conventions (using for instance as the day count 'actual'/360 for Treasuries, defining the number of trading days as opening days for TARGET and so on). Starting in January 1999, not only have all new issues been in euros, but all outstanding issues have been re-denominated (Danthine et al., 1999).

The *private debt market* has followed a similar process of rapid integration. As early as mid-June 1996, private interest rates in Belgium, France, Germany and the Netherlands had already converged. The market for primary corporate bond issues has also become more integrated, at least for the large firms, with new issues now placed all over Europe. The one billion euro issue of the French telecommunications group Alcatel, illustrates this point: 28% was sold, in February 1999, to Italian investors.

The integration of the European *banking industry* is of particular concern. For a long time the banking industry seemed at a standstill, with negligible cross-border banking. According to White (1998), cross-border offices within the EU represented only 0.3% of the total banking offices. Recently, however, merger movements have been spectacular.

- Domestic mergers between banks and between banks and insurance companies have soared (Banco Santander-Central Hispano, BBV-Argentaria, BNP-Paribas, San Paolo-IMI, INAI-Banco di Napoli, Intesa, Unicredito, HypoVereinsbank, ABN-Amro, Lloyds-TSB, SEB-Trygg-Hansa, Unidanmark-Tryg Baltica, among others).

- Cross-country mergers are, however, still quite limited and typically restricted to neighbouring countries (like the Merita-Nordbanken, or the BSCH-Champalimaud mergers).

These events reflect two somewhat unexpected phenomena. Mergers have occurred mainly within countries, while many had expected synergies to be larger across countries. Also, national regulatory authorities have stopped certain mergers. Examples at the cross-country level include the attempt by Spanish BSCH to acquire a controlling stake in the Champalimaud group, and the French regulatory authorities stopping foreign banks from taking over any French bank in the complex SG-BNP-Paribas deal. Regulators have blocked domestic mergers in both France and Italy.

Overall, European banks continue to be home based with limited operations in other European countries. Yet this could change with the next wave of mergers, which will inevitably be cross-border involving large banks.

2

Monetary stability

Throughout the year, speeches and reports from the ECB have emphasized the 'two-pillar approach' and the 'stability-oriented monetary policy strategy'. In this chapter we first review the words and deeds of the ECB in its first year of operation, asking whether these concepts can be given a more precise meaning. To sharpen our vision of the year, we use simulations to compare the behaviour of the ECB with that of other central banks, and to interpret the evolution of long-term interest rates. Overall, we find that the picture of the ECB strategy is still foggy. Next, we discuss the loaded issues of transparency and accountability. We take due account of the existing institutional arrangements to understand the main differences of opinion between the ECB and its critics, most clearly revealed in the Buiter–Issing debate. We conclude that the ECB differs from other independent central banks not just because of traditions in central banking, but also because of the peculiarities of the process of European integration that rub off on the design of its institutions.

2.1 The stability-oriented strategy in light of 1999

Observers and critics have raised many questions about the ECB and its chosen strategy for monetary policy. In pursuing its medium-term objective of keeping HIPC inflation between 0 and 2%, what weights will the ECB attach to its inflation forecast, relative to its reference value for M3 growth? Will the ECB pursue inflation forecast targeting in disguise, or will it treat the 0–2 % interval as a zone of inaction, attaching more significance to realized inflation? What weight – if any – will be put on output growth relative to inflation? Is the ECB going to continue the Bundesbank practice of paying attention to the exchange rate, or will it follow the US Federal Reserve's approach of benign neglect? And will the ECB confine its attention to the developments in individual Euroland countries and their impact on European averages, or will it give additional weight to important member countries and extreme single-country events?

Observing the policy of the ECB during just one year is clearly not long enough to answer any of these questions. In the following we therefore discuss not only the policy stance, but also the communication of the ECB; in addition, we try to fill the vacuum of lacking data with some counterfactual simulations.

Deeds and words – a first look

Speeches and documents, since the launch of the two-pillar strategy last fall, have emphasized that the ECB will concentrate on the medium-term outlook for prices. By following an approach of coarse tuning, rather than fine tuning, the ECB can afford to pay little attention to short-run output developments. Yet, the April 1999 cut in the policy rate of 50 basis points, to 2.5%, coincided with declining prospects for output in Euroland. (The previous 30 point cut to 3.0% in December 1998 was associated with deflationary risks in the wake of the Asian crisis.) In its explanation, however, the ECB stated that it was not concerned with growth or unemployment.

Similarly, after launching its two-pillar strategy the ECB has given constant prominence to the target – or reference value – for M3 growth, which has been set at 4.5% for 1999. The President and other Executive Board members stress this second pillar in their speeches. And the *Monthly Bulletin* devotes a great deal of space to current monetary developments, compared with current developments in prices – let alone the outlook for future inflation. Yet, in April, actual money growth was running at a rate above 5%. The ECB engaged in elaborate explanations of why the cut in rates was not a departure from the two-pillar strategy. This re-fuelled previous speculation that the role of money is to create a smokescreen, which matters little when priorities must be made *vis-à-vis* the final objectives of inflation and output, but can provide a formal rationalization for a sensitive policy decision.[1]

At this point, the ECB for the first time had to face what some of its critics had said all along: an imprecise statement of the strategy might be a mixed blessing. While imprecision may give some leeway or discretion, it creates a communication problem when monetary developments point in a different direction than other policy-relevant information.

As the outlook for output and prices turned upward in the summer, money growth edged up further: the September figure

---

1. Many observers have suggested that this is the way the Bundesbank used money targets in the past. Indeed, recent empirical evaluations of Bundesbank behaviour stress how intermediate money-growth targets were often missed and given low priority when a conflict arose with the final inflation objective (see von Hagen (1995) and Clarida and Gertler (1997)).

was already above 6%. The common direction of all these indicators made it easier for the ECB to explain the 4 November hike in the interest rate by 50 basis points, bringing the policy rate back to 3.0%. But referring to several indicators makes it harder for outside observers to pinpoint how ECB weighs inflation and output. Of course, one can treat money as a smokescreen, as some market watchers apparently did: 'if the ECB needed a final reason to hike, they have it' (*Financial Times*, 28 October 1999). Taking the words of the ECB seriously, however, the simple truth is that it is much more difficult to form an opinion about two relative weights (forecast inflation vs. output and vs. money) than about one.

ECB opaqueness is less to blame for suspicions among observers that ECB decisions will disproportionately respond to developments in certain countries. On the contrary, statements that interest rates will only respond to the average macroeconomic developments in Euroland have been crystal clear. This is indeed the appropriate stance, but the ECB has become overcautious, coming close to stepping over the brink of distorting self-censorship. The fact that the spring downturn in economic conditions was centred on Germany and Italy is a likely explanation for the ECB's reluctance to admit any concern for output and unemployment in its explanation of the April cut in interest rates. On a similar note, the ECB does not publish data on individual countries, arguing that this would be misleading, as policy should not be directed at country-specific situations. (Duisenberg, hearings at the European Parliament 26 October 1999.) This is somewhat ridiculous, as these data are already given a lot of prominence in the public debate. Credible communication about current and future developments in Euroland must be allowed to touch upon the separate parts that go into the average.

In summary, the way the ECB has chosen to communicate its intentions and its decisions has not always contributed to resolving the outstanding questions about the meaning of its strategy.

2.2 Assessing the first year of ECB policy

Evaluating the performance of the two-pillar strategy during the first year of EMU would be very interesting. But such evaluation is virtually impossible as it is well established that the effects of monetary policy on inflation are observed with long lags, certainly longer than one year. Of course we can always look at monetary aggregates, but a classic problem (technically known as the identification problem) arises: is money growth driven by supply or by demand? This problem is particularly severe in the present case where we face a completely new monetary regime in the euro area, which

Figure 2.1 Output gaps (EUGAP), actual inflation (EUINFL) and one-year-ahead expected inflation (EUINFL_F) in the euro area

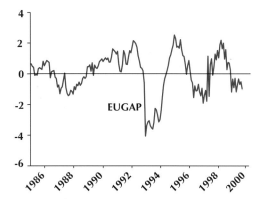

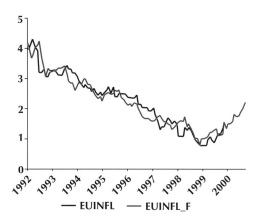

— EUINFL — EUINFL_F

prevents us from looking at past regularities in ECB behaviour to evaluate its actions with respect to its stated goals. It is possible, however, to ask one meaningful question: how differently from the ECB would a central bank with known historical characteristics have behaved if faced with the same conditions?

How does the ECB compare to the Fed and Buba?

As a natural benchmark, we use the behaviour of successful central banks, the US Federal Reserve (Fed) – a central bank that also operates in a large and fairly closed economy – and the German Bundesbank (Buba) – an obvious yardstick given the history of EMU. We encapsulate these central banks' historical behaviour in the form of a forward-looking Taylor rule, a tool of analysis further described in Box 2.1. The Taylor rule considers that central banks set their policy interest rates in response to the evolution of just two variables: the output gap (the deviation of output from its trend) and the inflation gap (the deviation of forecast from targeted inflation.) This rule has proved to be quite powerful in interpreting monetary policies in several countries, including the US and Germany

Of crucial importance are the weights that the central bank assigns to each of the two targets, output and inflation. Our estimates of the Fed and Buba weights are reported in Box 2.1. Unsurprisingly, the Fed is found to be relatively more sensitive to the output gap than the Buba. The Box also explains how we estimate the output gaps and expected inflation for the US, Germany and Euroland. The Euroland output gap and expected inflation during the last year are depicted in Figure 2.1.

BOX 2.1 The Taylor rule

We use a forward-looking Taylor rule, a tool designed to analyse central bank behaviour, following the work of Clarida, Gali, and Gertler (1998).[1] It assumes that the policy interest rate R is set over time according to the following formula:

$$R_t^* = \alpha_0 + \alpha_1(\pi_{t+12}^e - \pi^*) + \alpha_2(y_t - y^*)$$

The first bracketed term is the gap between twelve-month ahead forecast inflation and the inflation target and the second is the output gap. Actual rates are assumed to adjust slowly towards these equilibrium rates. Estimation requires that we measure these two gaps. The output gaps are obtained using deviations of the log of industrial production from trend (obtained by applying the Hodrick-Prescott filter), while one-year ahead expected inflation is obtained by using the historical dependence of observed inflation on current output gap, current Euro-inflation and current commodity-price inflation.[2] With this methodology, we estimate policy rules for the Buba and the Fed, using monthly data for the period 1987–9. We obtain the coefficients $\alpha_1 = 1.3$, $\alpha_2 = 0.2$ for the Buba, and $\alpha_1 = 1.0$, $\alpha_2 = 0.9$ for the Fed, indicating a more vigorous output response by the Fed. These estimates are well in line with earlier results, as well as popular perception.

In the simulation we treat expected inflation and the output gap as exogenous. This is appropriate in a simulation stretching over a single year, as the lags in monetary policy mean that policy affects macroeconomic variables only at horizons above one year.

1. This tool was used already in the first *MECB* report (Begg et al., 1998).
2. We experimented by adding M3 growth to the set of instruments, but it never turned out to be significant.

Equipped with Taylor rules for the Fed and the Buba (i.e. a measure of their historical preferences), we can next ask how these central banks would have set their policy interest rates over the last 12 months if faced with the euro area output and inflation gaps. The simulations are reported in Figure 2.2. Neither the Fed nor the Buba Taylor rule is able to explain the cut by 50 basis points in early April. According to the simulations, these central banks would have both delivered an EONIA rate somewhere between 3.0 and 3.5 per cent throughout the year. The 50 basis point hike in early November brought the observed rate closer to the predicted paths.

The falling Euro output gap in the first half of the year is thus not enough to explain the expansionary policy stance adopted then. This would require a considerably stronger output response than the already high one estimated for the Fed. Despite the ECB's declarations of a coarse-tuning strategy, these simulations thus portray a quite activist strategy. A caveat is in order though. A strong output response need not reflect policy activism: the responsiveness of interest rates to macroeconomic conditions estimated in the Taylor Rule depends not only on the central bank's preferences over inflation and output, but also on how the economy responds to monetary policy.

Euroland aggregates or not?

An alternative explanation for the expansionary policy in the spring is that the ECB paid special attention to the parts of the euro area – Germany and Italy – which were facing a cyclical slowdown. To shed light on this alternative, we ask what would have been the Buba's policy had it been in charge of Germany and Italy – we assign a weight of 0.65 to Germany's macroeconomic conditions and of 0.35 to Italy's. Now, the simulation displayed in Figure 2.3 tracks very closely the actual interest rate. In this interpretation, the ECB claims to look only at averages, but it acts differently; deeds do not quite match words.

Is it monetary targeting?

To shed further light on the ECB's deeds, we turn to money growth, the second pillar of its announced strategy. We start with the polar case where the ECB would follow a pure monetary-targeting strategy, with the ultimate purpose of controlling inflation between 1 and 2%. A money-targeting central bank also adjusts its interest rate to the output gap and deviations of actual inflation from target, taking into account how money demand reacts to changes in output and the interest rate.

The question of money demand in Europe, and its stability, lies at the heart of criticism of the second pillar. With no history to rely upon, we do not know the behaviour of money demand in the euro area, but then, how can the ECB perform monetary

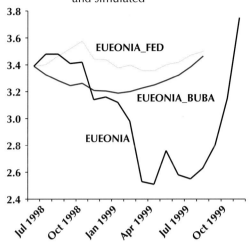

Figure 2.2   ECB monetary policy, actual and simulated

Actual interest rate: EUEONIA
Interest rate simulating Fed monetary policy: EUEONIA_FED
Interest rate simulating Bundesbank monetary policy: EUEONIA_BUBA.
The simulations use our estimates of the Fed's and the Bundesbank's reactions to one-year-ahead expected inflation and current output gaps in euro-wide area.

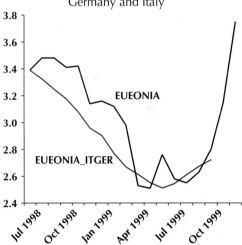

Figure 2.3   ECB monetary policy aiming at Germany and Italy

Actual interest rate: EUEONIA
Interest rate simulating Bundesbank policy aiming at a weighted average of German and Italian macroeconomic conditions: EUEONIA_ITGER (weights, 0.65 and 0.35, respectively).

Figure 2.4   Monetary-targeting policy

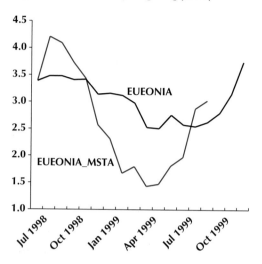

Actual interest rate: EUEONIA
Interest rate simulating a policy of targeting a three-month moving average of annual rate of growth of M3: EUEONIA_MSTA.

Figure 2.5   The two-pillar strategy

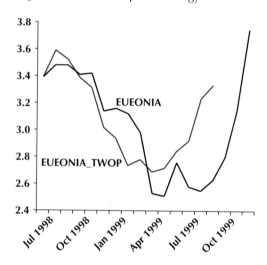

Actual interest rate: EUEONIA
Interest rate simulating a monetary policy based on a two-pillar strategy: EUEONIA_TWOP.
The two-pillar strategy is simulated as a weighted average of the forward-looking Taylor rule (with coefficients estimated on Buba behaviour) and the strict money-targeting rule, where the weights of 0.72 on the Taylor rule and 0.28 on the money rule have been chosen to minimize the (squared) distance between simulated and actual rates.

growth targeting? We ignore this important issue by adopting estimates of money demand behaviour in the euro area reported in a recent working paper issued by the ECB (Coenen and Vega, 1999): the elasticity of demand for M3 relative to output is set at 1.17, and relative to the interest rate at –1.26. In keeping with ECB practice, we compute changes in money as a three-month moving average.

Figure 2.4 reports the simulated behaviour of a pure money-targeting ECB over the course of 1999. Here the simulated interest rate reacts more vigorously than the actual rate. In the spring, it is cut sharply to about 1.5%, even though actual money growth is above target, because money demand is falling rapidly as the output gap deteriorates. When output and money demand pick up speed in the summer, the rate is raised back towards 3%. Thus, the simulation traces well the direction of the two policy shifts in 1999, even though it is way off in quantitative terms. Unlike the previous simulation, the real ECB does not act as aggressively as the simulated, pure money-targeting ECB would!

A two-pillar strategy after all?

If the ECB's actions are correctly predicted by a one-pillar strategy as far as the direction and timing of moves is concerned, but not as far as the size of the moves, could the announced two-pillar strategy be the right interpretation? To explore that possibility we simulate the policy of a central bank that partly follows a forward-looking Taylor rule (using the preferences based on Buba behaviour) representing the second pillar, and partly a strict money-targeting rule representing the monetary pillar. We still need to specify how much weight the central bank ascribes to each of the two pillars. In order to give the maximum chance to this interpretation, we choose the relative weights so as to minimise the (squared) distance between the simulated and actual interest rates. This gives a weight of 72% for the Taylor rule and 28% for the money rule. As Figure 2.5 shows, the simulated two-pillar strategy does about as well as the Taylor rule based on Italian and German macroeconomic conditions in tracking the actual data.

Well, who knows?

Thus, among the various interpretations of ECB behaviour that we have proposed, the two most successful specifications are those that the ECB might indicate as the best (two-pillar) and the worst (exclusive focus on Germany and Italy) model for describing its behaviour. This gives additional force to the argument we made at the end of Section 2.1. On the basis of its deeds and words to date, it is extremely hard to judge what kind of animal the ECB is.

1999 – another inflation scare?

The difficulty in reconstructing ECB behaviour is not just a source of frustration for ECB watchers. It leaves the markets uncertain about the strategy that will be followed next. While such market uncertainty may leave the ECB with some discretion, it also carries costs. The market may charge an additional risk premium, particularly in the medium-run maturity segment, which is highly sensitive to expectations about policy over the next few years. For this reason, it is interesting to consider data from financial markets in the past year.

While 1999 may have been a rather boring year for inflation, it has been more interesting for longer-term interest rates. These rates are a useful source of information in that they reflect the expectations by market participants about future policy, both directly, through the 'expectations hypothesis,' and indirectly, through expected exchange rates and inflation.

Figure 2.6 depicts the yield-to maturity of 10-year benchmark bonds for the US, UK and Germany over the period 1993–9. We take German long-term rates to capture 10-year yields in the euro area (default premia for other Eurobonds have been low in 1999 with small fluctuations in the 15–25 basis point range). We bring UK rates into the picture for two reasons. The UK is a prominent European non-EMU member and the Bank of England has undergone a regime change when, in May 1997, the Government gave the Bank operational responsibility for setting interest rates, a move confirmed by the Bank of England Act, coming into force in June 1998.

As indicated by the two shaded areas in Figure 2.6, the path for 1999 bond yields closely resembles the situation in 1994. This is interesting, because the 1994 rise in US bond yields reflect an 'inflation scare' (Goodfriend, 1993). Actual inflation in 1994 and thereafter never matched the expectations implicit in the steeper yield curve. Moreover, the inflation scare had a contagious effect on European markets, where the long-term bond yields rose in the course of 1994. Interestingly, the reaction of UK bond yields was more than proportional to the rise in US yields, whereas the reaction of German yields was exactly proportional to this rise. Figure 2.7 reports annualized inflation rates in the US (the CPI), the euro area (the HIPC), and the UK (the RPIX): while US inflation did not take off in 1994, European inflation was actually declining.

Clearly, realized inflation also reflects the effect of realized policy. In 1994, monetary policy was restrictive in the US, but expansionary in continental Europe. In the UK, policy was neutral in the first part of the year, but became restrictive in the later part. The policy rates (the US Fed funds rate, the German call money rate, and the UK base rate) are plotted in Figure 2.8. On the basis of these asynchronized policies, many observers expected a 'decoupling' of European and US long-term bond yields. As Figure

Figure 2.6 Long-term yields

Figure 2.7 Inflation

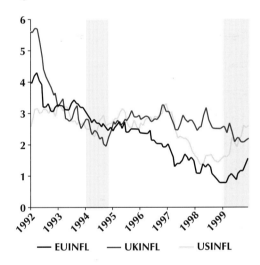

Figure 2.8 Policy rates

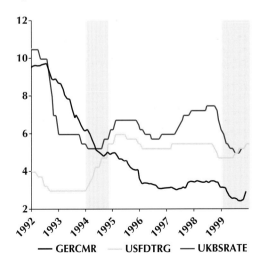

2.6 reveals, however, the bond yields continued to follow each other. In fact, European long-term yields started declining as soon as the progressive increase of the federal fund target from 3% to 6% eventually managed to defeat the inflation scare.

A possible explanation for the close association between European and US rates in 1994 (according to uncovered interest parity) is that markets did not expect long-term fluctuations in European–US exchange rates. This would be consistent with monetary policies characterized by a 'benign neglect' of the exchange rate on the part of the Fed and by a preference for exchange rate stabilization on the part of the European banks.

Our own estimate of expected inflation in Europe – shown in Figure 2.1 (page 20) – gives some support to this idea. Indeed we have found that US inflation is leading European inflation, with a one-for-one effect in the long run. This can only be reconciled with the long-run validity of PPP if the dollar–euro (or DM) exchange rate is expected to be stable in the long run. The more than proportional reaction of UK yields cannot be explained by uncovered interest parity alone, though. But it can plausibly be attributed to a contagion from the US inflation scare to a higher UK risk premium reflecting low Bank of England credibility.

What does all this tell us about 1999? It can shed light on the crucial question of credibility. Monetary institutions have changed in Europe with the introduction of the ECB and the independence of the Bank of England. Have they changed the picture? 1999 saw a rise in US interest rates resembling that of five years earlier. And there have been fears of higher actual US inflation while European inflation held steady during the first ten months of the year. Yet European long-term rates once again tended to follow US rates, but the reaction appears weaker than in 1994.

Can we say more precisely whether the observed response of European bond rates to the surge in US rates changed between 1994 and 1999? To answer this question, we again use past behaviour to produce a counterfactual simulation for 1999. Using weekly averages of daily data, we have estimated the historical dependence of UK and German bond yields on US long-term bond yields over two periods: the first ten months of 1994 and the first ten months of 1999.[2] We use this relationship to analyse the responses of UK and German long-term rates to US rates in 1999. Figures 2.9 and 2.10 each reports three curves. One is the actual development of the UK or German long-term rate in 1999. The second curve, closely tracking the former, is the simulated response of the European rate to the US rate,

2. It is indeed appropriate to treat US long-term interest rates as exogenous in the estimation, as these are identifiable as the common trend in fluctuations of European and US rates over the period we consider. Both German and UK models are estimated as unrestricted Error Correction specifications. Full specifications are available upon request.

when we use the behaviour estimated over 1999. The third and uppermost curve shows the counterfactual obtained by simulating the response of European yields to observed US 1999 yields, when we use the behaviour estimated over 1994. These figures confirm that 1999 has witnessed another instance of contagion in bond markets, but the effect is definitely more limited than in 1994.

It is tempting to interpret the UK counterfactual as an enhancement of Bank of England credibility. Matters are different for the ECB, though. The ECB – unlike the Buba – is the central bank of an economy comparable in size and openness to that of the US. Thus, the 1994 explanation based on Fed benign neglect and Buba concern for exchange-rate stability should no longer apply, and we could have expected euro rates not to be seriously affected by the inflation scare in the US. While the US influence over the euro rate is indeed reduced, it still is of about the same magnitude as for the Bank of England.

This seems to suggest that the markets are not yet fully convinced that the ECB will treat the euro–dollar exchange rate with benign neglect. Ambiguous statements by the Executive Board, and uncertainty on the ECB monetary policy strategy, are the most obvious explanation for the persistent correlation between US and Euro yields. This can be seen as the cost of ambiguity.

Summary

Our observations of ECB's deeds and words in 1999, backed by our counterfactual simulations, suggest that much remains to be done to communicate the precise meaning of the announced monetary policy strategy. Unless the ECB clarifies its intentions it will take time – possibly a lot of time – for outside observers to form a clear view. Meanwhile, markets are left to guess, and to price the risk. Uncertainty also breeds speculative debates about what is happening inside the meeting room of the ECB Governing Council. We now turn to these issues, starting with the emerging modes of communication and decision-making.

2.3 Transparency and accountability

In its first year of operation, the ECB has drawn a great deal of criticism for its communication with the public, its analyses, policy deliberations and interest-rate decisions. Many have complained about a lack of transparency and accountability. The ECB President and other members of the Executive Board are strongly defending the emerging procedures. According to them, the ECB has not only gone further than obliged by the statutes laid out by the Treaty, but it has also become one of the most transparent and accountable central banks in the world. The difference of views is clearly

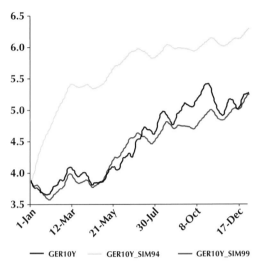

Figure 2.9   Responses of German long-term rates to US long-term rates in 1999

Actual long-term rate: GER10Y
Long-term rate simulation using the model fitted on 1999 data: GER10Y_SIM99
Long-term rate simulation using the model fitted on 1994 data: GER10Y_SIM94

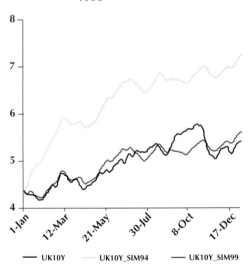

Figure 2.10   Responses of UK long-term rates to US long-term rates in 1999

Actual long-term rate: UK10Y94
Long-term rate simulation using the model fitted on 1999 data: UK10Y_SIM99
Long-term rate simulation using the model fitted on 1994 data: UK10Y_SIM94

revealed in the debate between Otmar Issing, ECB Executive Board member and Chief Economist, and Willem Buiter, an external member of the Monetary Policy Committee of the Bank of England (Buiter, 1999a, and Issing, 1999). Both advocate the procedures of their own institutions, on the same grounds of transparency and accountability.

Clearly then, the two sides in the debate must mean different things when using these terms. Indeed the discussion about transparency and accountability has many facets. It is convenient to split the issues in two. In this section we discuss communication with the market and decision making, taking the existing institutions laid down by the Treaty as given. The next section deals with the longer-run issues of institution design and political legitimacy.

A common starting point

Both the academic literature[3] and practical policy experience have fostered a broad consensus on the desirable framework for monetary policy. The credibility of the commitment to low inflation is recognized as crucial in providing a long-run anchor for inflationary expectations. Credibility, in turn, requires that monetary policy be at arms-length distance from short-run political pressure. And central banks should be given the instrument independence necessary to achieve price stability.

Although this may have been controversial ten years ago, it is now conventional wisdom. Most observers would also agree that it is important that monetary policy be predictable in the short to medium run, as this contributes to market stability. Predictability is enhanced by systematic behaviour, which makes it important for policymakers to build a reputation. Predictability is not only enhanced by systematic decisions, but also by public understanding. This makes effective communication with the market desirable.

Both sides of the ECB debate would agree on these generalities but, as usual, the devil is in the detail. Proponents of the Bank of England model and of the ECB model vehemently disagree on how a central bank should best communicate its strategy to the market (transparency about policy) and report on its deliberations and policy decisions (accountability). As we shall see, these disagreements also lead to different conclusions on how central banks can build their reputations.

Communication about policy – ex ante or ex post transparency?

In the course of the last few years, the Bank of England has

---

3. Persson and Tabellini (2000) survey the theory, while Eijffinger and de Haan (1996) summarise empirical studies.

gradually developed a specific model of communication, which can be labelled the *ex ante* approach. The basic idea is to openly discuss contingency plans for policy. The discussion relies on detailed and numerical accounts of the forecast distributions for inflation and output: the famous fan charts in the quarterly *Inflation Report* fulfil this purpose. Policy is explicitly geared toward keeping forecast inflation close to its target, without inducing too large fluctuations in output or employment. Policy changes are thus explained as deriving from revisions of the forecast distributions in the light of incoming information.

The stated philosophy behind this approach to transparency and communication is to make the discussion about monetary policy a 'technical issue' (see King (1997) and Buiter (1999b)). An open discussion about monetary policy is welcome as long it takes place in accordance with the ground rules of the Bank's strategy. Even though the policy decisions may have a bearing on short-run conflicts with political dimensions, a proponent of a more expansionary policy must explain why this enhances the likelihood of hitting the inflation target down the line, given existing information. An important prerequisite for this approach, to which we will return shortly, is that the central bank has *instrument* independence, but not *goal* independence.[4]

Another – and quite different – model of communication about policy is associated with the Buba. It has also become the ECB model in its first year of operation. It can be labelled the *ex post* approach. Here, communication is mostly backward looking, rather than forward looking. Thus, written reports and speeches focus on current and past information and do not contain the Central Bank's forecasts, as is the case with the *Monthly Bulletin*. Similarly, alternative courses for policy are not discussed openly ahead of time. Policy decisions are instead explained once they have been made, sometimes with reference to money growth being out of range, sometimes in terms of looming risks for inflation. Thus the ECB sees the monthly press conferences as a means of rationalizing the decisions taken in past meetings of the Governing Council, not as a means of outlining future policies.

In one sense, the motive for this approach to communication is similar to the motive for the *ex ante* approach. Both recognise that the future course of monetary policy can easily become politically contentious, and seek to avoid public discussion of the politics of policy. But the ECB like the Buba previously, has not only instrument independence, but also considerable goal independence. It has not been given any precise numerical objective, formulated elsewhere, only the Treaty's general appeal to price stability. Thus it is much harder to appeal to a technical

---

4. The distinction between instrument independence and goal independence was introduced by Fischer (1995) and is related to the earlier distinction between economic and political independence suggested by Grilli, Masciandaro and Tabellini (1991).

Table 2.1 Transparency of policy

	Goal Independence	Policy Target	Numerical Target	Projections	Policy publication
European Central Bank	yes	no	no	no	monthly
Federal Reserve Bank	yes	no	no	1-2 year estimates	semi-annual
Bank of Japan	yes	no	no	no	monthly
Bank of England	no	inflation	yes	2 year probability distribution	quarterly
Bank of Canada	mixed	inflation.	yes	no	semi-annual
Sverige Riksbank	yes	inflation.	yes	2 year probability distribution	quarterly
Bank of Israel	no	inflation.	yes	no	semi-annual
Reserve Bank of Australia	mixed	inflation.	yes	2 year external estimates	quarterly
Reserve Bank of New Zealand	mixed	inflation.	yes	2-3 year estimates	quarterly

task of implementation in discussing the future course of policy. Instead the Council deems it better to simply abstain from such forward-looking discussion and puts policy behind a smokescreen.

How do other independent central banks behave in comparison with these two archetypes? The Fed sits somewhere in between, probably closer to the *ex post* approach of the ECB. Like the ECB it has some goal independence and does not discuss future policy decisions with reference to a specific numerical target and does not publish its forecasts. But the discussion of future policy, particularly by the Chairman of the Board of Governors, is more forward-looking than in the case of the ECB. Table 2.1 summarises information about current practice among instrument-independent central banks. Practices vary among other central banks, with the Swedish Riksbank and the Reserve Bank of New Zealand aligned with the Bank of England and the Bank of Japan aligned with the ECB.

What factors other than goal independence might explain the different approaches in the UK and EMU? One is the obvious Bundesbank heritage. Also, the predominant central bank tradition has historically been much closer to the ECB's *ex post* approach. The transformation in the UK is perhaps the bigger mystery, particularly in view of the long obsession with secrecy in British politics. Another possible factor is the previous professional experience of ECB policy-makers. Most of the members of the first Governing Council made their careers in central banks operating under a fixed exchange rate regime, where discussing future policy plans in public was an absolute taboo, given the risks of destabilizing currency speculation.

Committee decisions – individual or collective accountability?

Virtually all instrument-independent central banks set their policy instruments in a committee that makes decisions by majority rule. This way of making decisions has two consequences.

First, it allows for the *aggregation of information*. Even if all committee members share the same objective, they may still come to different conclusions about the right course of policy because they have alternative pieces of information about the economy, or different ways of interpreting existing information. Pooling the information of several members through voting on policy will lead to better outcomes, on average, than decisions by a single policy-maker. In addition, ill-informed members of the committee might rationally abstain from taking a strong stand on policy and let the better informed members decide rather than unwittingly tilting the vote outcome in a particular direction.[5]

Second, committee decisions allow for the *aggregation of different interests*. This suggests a more conventional rationale for the common practice. Monetary policy affects the real economy in the short to medium run through temporary effects on relative prices and incomes. Different groups in society thus have conflicting short-run policy preferences. These can be balanced against each other in a committee, provided the groups are represented.[6]

Committee decision-making raises the issue of how the central bank should be held accountable for its decisions. To a large degree, accountability is exercised through institutional provisions outside the bank's control (the specific provisions for the ECB are discussed more closely in the next section). But accountability also hinges on the bank's own reporting of its deliberations and decisions. On this point, we can again identify two very different models.

One is the model of *individual* accountability. It is associated with the reformed Bank of England. Individual votes on policy are disclosed with a short lag (presently two weeks). Minutes of committee meetings discuss differences in individual assessments. Although different views are not attributed to individual members, combining the minutes with the voting record makes it possible to identify who said what – at least in those cases when it mattered. Similarly, the *Inflation Report* openly discusses differences in individual views on the forecast. Moreover, by design, members of the Monetary Policy Committee have relatively short, three-year, terms and there are no limits to reappointment.

The rationale underlying this approach is essentially the same as the rationale underlying the *ex ante* approach to communication: the absence of goal independence. The bank's principal, namely the Government, takes a political decision specifying the precise objective for monetary policy in the form

---

5. These results are inspired by the theory of information aggregation, which has its roots in the works by the Marquis de Condorcet, and has recently been revived by theorists in economics and political science – see Piketty (1999) for a survey of recent work. Applications to monetary policy could have high pay-offs, but are still lacking in the literature.
6. A small body of theoretical and empirical work has applied insights from the theory of majority decisions in committees to this aspect of monetary policy (see Begg et al. (1998) for some references).

of a numerical inflation target. Given this, monetary policy becomes a technical issue. Drawing on the discussion above, the committee's role is to aggregate information into policy. All that then matters is the quality of an individual committee member's analysis and reappointment to the committee is a natural reward for revealed competence and good work (given the lags in monetary policy, however, three years may be too short a time to systematically judge the quality of the analysis). Individual accountability takes care of prospective temptations for obfuscation in information acquisition and transmission; when members are judged on an individual basis, each of them has strong incentives to find out and tell the truth. But even the sun has spots. Individual members of the Monetary Policy Committee generally refrain from publicly discussing their personal views on future policy, and are not allowed to disclose dissenting views until the votes have been published.

The alternative is *collective* accountability, the approach of the ECB – and the Buba before it. No individual votes are disclosed and no minutes reveal individual differences. The monthly press conference following the policy meetings of the Governing Council sticks to the decision made by the majority and does not report on dissenting views. It is also interesting to note the rules for reappointment, which are of course beyond the control of the ECB. Each NCB has its own rules, but governor terms must have a minimum duration of five years and can generally be renewed. The eight-year terms for the Executive Board, however, are not renewable.

The collective accountability approach, as the *ex post* approach to transparency, has its roots in the considerable goal independence of the ECB. The framers of the Maastricht Treaty were defining the Governing Council's task partly as a political one, namely to implicitly formulate the precise objectives for policy. Appointment rules to the Governing Council were made consistent with this decision. The Council is there to aggregate conflicting short-run interests into policy. Thus, its composition reflects a balance of different interests – in this case exclusively national interests (more on this in the next section). As this highlights the political dimension of the task, it was deemed logical to insist on long terms, and to limit the possibility of re-appointment to limit the levers for political pressure. The ban on instructions to Council members serves a similar purpose. This absence from political control also serves, however, to strengthen the goal independence of the ECB.

Given this design, it is not surprising that many observers view the Council's task as one of balancing different national interests and are led to speculate about greater weight given to certain countries. The Council acutely recognises this view, and takes every possible step to avoid the political tension associated with open policy conflict. Decisions are thus made behind the closed doors of the Governing Council's meeting-room. No

Table 2.2   Accountability of policy-making committees

	release of minutes	current lag of release	record of votes	individual views
European Central Bank	no	-	-	-
Federal Reserve Bank	yes	6 weeks	identified	yes, identified
Bank of Japan	yes	4 weeks	identified	yes, identified
Bank of England	yes	2 weeks	identified	yes, not identified
Bank of Canada	yes	5 weeks	no	no
Sverige Riksbank	yes	2 weeks	mentioned	yes, identified
Bank of Israel	no	-	-	-
Reserve Bank of Australia	no	-	-	-
Reserve Bank of New Zealand	no	-	-	-

records of individual votes or minutes that report on different views are published. Information is confined to a single message: if different members are viewed as having conflicting interests, they may also be suspected of using information strategically. The rationale for the collective approach to accountability is the same as the rationale for the *ex post* approach to communication. The Council feels that reporting on individual views and votes would open the same can of political worms as would open *ex ante* discussion of alternative courses of policy.

Other central banks have different rules for reporting their deliberations and decisions. Most banks fall quite neatly into either the collective or individual accountability model. The design of the US Fed reflects an original concern for the balancing of different interests (see Faust, 1996, and Begg et al., 1998). But nowadays the Fed does report on individual differences: votes are disclosed within six weeks, together with minutes. In addition, the Chairman has a special role and is generally held individually accountable for the success or failure of Fed policy. Table 2.2 summarises the current practice of instrument-independent central banks.

Summary

Our discussion about transparency and accountability can be summarized graphically. The simple two-dimensional graph shown in Figure 2.11 combines the information in Tables 2.1 and 2.2. It is perhaps no coincidence that Messrs Issing and Buiter disagree. The position of the Bank of England and the ECB in each dimension has its roots in the different institutional ramifications of the two institutions. The Monetary Policy Committee views itself as a set of individuals appointed for the technical task of implementing a political decision made elsewhere. The Governing Council instead views itself – or, rather, strongly suspects that others view it – as a set of representatives appointed for making a balanced decision on a politically contentious policy issue.

Figure 2.11 Transparency and accountability

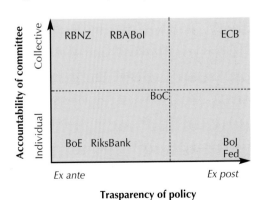

Note: The qualitative information contained in Tables 2.1 and 2.2 has been coded into numerical values to produce the above graph (precise coding is available upon request).

Does it matter for reputations and market stability?

What are the consequences of alternative approaches to transparency and accountability? In particular, which arrangements are likely to make policy more predictable in the short to medium run and hence reduce volatility and risk premiums in the bond market? One aspect of this question concerns the pace of learning by financial markets and other observers. Learning how to accurately predict the behaviour of the central bank is likely to be more rapid with an *ex ante* approach to transparency. It is easier to learn how to predict future policy, when the bank is specific about which variables govern the course of policy and reveals its best judgement of the future path of these variables in quantitative terms.

If instead the bank's communication focuses on *ex post* explanations, market participants have to rely more heavily on interpreting actual policy decisions. This will be a harder task, particularly if the bank is not very specific about which variables mean most for its decisions. What comes to mind is the situation in the 1980s when market participants were shifting back and forth between different indicator variables believed to exert particular influence on Fed policy – money, the stock market, the dollar, or the US external balance. This kind of situation would be particularly bad for a new and untested institution.

Learning by market participants creates opportunities for central bankers to build reputations for consistent behaviour and reputations can be an important asset in building and preserving credibility. The transparency approach may affect the way reputations are built. With an *ex post* approach market participants largely have to rely on observing the bank's actions. With an *ex ante* approach the bank's decisions can be measured against its previous announcements. This matching of deeds against words might allow for stronger enforcement and hence promote greater stability of market expectations about future policy. More effective learning about policy also gives stronger incentives for the bank to build a reputation.[7]

How is learning and reputation-building affected by the approach to accountability? This issue is not yet well understood, but let us offer some conjectures.[8] In the Bank of England approach, reputations become naturally tied to the individual members of the Monetary Policy Committee – the *Financial Times'* 'aviary indexes' of policy orientation and activism can be thought of as evolving measures of those individual reputations. Translating a bunch of individual reputations to a likely decision on interest rates in a new policy situation may not, however, be an easy task. Renewal of the committee means that the market

---

7. This point is developed by Geerats (1999); see also Faust and Svensson (1999).
8. Sibert (1999) takes a first step towards modeling the distinction between individual and collective reputations in monetary policy.

has to learn afresh about the likely behaviour of new members. As each new member must build up their own reputation, the market is constantly learning about the likely direction of policy.

With collective accountability, the relevant concept becomes the collective reputation of the institution as a whole. It is reasonable to conjecture that it is easier for observers of the ECB to predict future policy behaviour from such a collective reputation, than from a set of 17 reputations of individual Council members. This feeds back into stronger collective incentives for maintaining a reputation – once it has been built – which, in turn, makes policy more stable. Furthermore, the collective reputation becomes like a 'corporate culture,' which may be more easily passed on to new members of the Governing Council.[9]

The histories of monetary policy-making in the US and Germany illustrate the distinction between individual and collective reputations. Many observers attribute recent successes in US policy to Chairmen such as Volcker and Greenspan rather than to the Fed as an institution. Conversely, past failures are attributed to Chairmen such as Miller and Burns. The continued success of German monetary policy, on the other hand, is more often attributed to the Buba as an institution than to the leadership of its Presidents – even though many Buba Presidents, such as Pöhl and Tietmeyer, certainly have been very strong personalities.

2.4 Institution design and political legitimacy

No central bank can operate successfully without the trust of the public. Weak institutions can get into serious trouble, as recent events in Europe have forcefully illustrated. The Commission is the only EU body with executive powers comparable to the ECB. Its trouble in the spring of 1999, led to a situation of acute crisis management which crippled the ability to deal with normal business. But such events may also have important long-run consequences. An institution that is perceived as non-legitimate becomes naturally defensive. It thus becomes afraid to take actions with long-run benefits, which can arouse short-run controversy – such as a forceful competition policy in the case of the Commission, or a stable monetary policy in the case of the ECB.

The ECB shares some peculiar features with other EU bodies, namely a rigid legal mandate, long chains of political delegation, and a nationally-oriented representation. These peculiar features are important when one tries to understand the channels through which the ECB can be held accountable. These channels in turn affect the way the ECB can earn and maintain its political legitimacy.

9. See Kreps (1990) and especially Tirole (1996).

Accountability through which channels?

All independent central banks have only conditional independence. This is at the core of democratic delegation: whenever a set of political principals delegates the power to carry out a certain task, they must have the ability to hold their common agent accountable for its performance. The ultimate sanction is a withdrawal of the legal mandate. Although this possibility is formally open, the mountainous difficulty in changing the Treaties of the European Union makes the ECB's mandate much less conditional than that of any national central bank.

In nation states the ultimate principals, namely the citizens, rely on their political representatives for monitoring and holding the central bank accountable. The particular structure of the ECB, however, makes these chains of delegation especially long and protracted. Reports to the ECOFIN public hearings in the European Parliament by the ECB, as well as reports and hearings at home with governors of the national central banks, certainly constitute valuable means of information. By the Treaty these bodies can give no instructions to the ECB, however, not even when it comes to its general goals, such as how to make operational the vague phrase of price stability. Moreover, there is no way in which a misbehaving Executive Board member or national governor can be fired. The monitoring by political representatives can thus only serve a highly limited role in the exercise of accountability. The result is the perception that the ECB is more goal-independent than other central banks, even though its function is quite strictly defined in the Maastricht Treaty. Its independence is essentially due to the absence of an effective political principal.

What remains is the power of appointment. The governments (parliament in the case of Finland) of the eleven member states each appoint the governor of its national central bank, who is assured a seat in the Governing Council. The six members of the Executive Board are appointed 'by common accord by the governments of the Member States' (Article 109a(2)(b)). Once again this provides a channel for national interests although, in this case, a balance of national interests is achieved through bargaining among the member countries.

Accountability to which constituencies?

We have argued that the approaches the ECB has adopted for communicating its policy and decision-making can be interpreted as a response to its goal independence and the perception that the Governing Council is appointed to balance short-run interests in monetary policy. The institutional design is consistent with this interpretation if we view the crucial conflicting interests in monetary policy as tied to national interests. It also ties in with the current debate in Europe. Yes, booming and busting member states in the EMU may have different views on the best monetary policy in the short run, but the Governing Council is designed to make precisely such judgements, finding the best compromise 'one shoe to fit all' monetary policy in the name of Europe.

But is this national conflict the most important political conflict in the short-run design of European monetary policy? This is far from clear. It may well be dominated by, say, the conflict between creditors and debtors regarding short-term real interest – debtors desiring more expansionary policies to cut their borrowing costs, and creditors desiring the opposite. Likewise, an important short-term conflict exists between insiders and outsiders in labour markets, as monetary policy can change real wages in the short run – insiders preferring restrictive policies giving higher real incomes and outsiders preferring lower real wages and better opportunities of finding a job. These groups form broad coalitions across the borders of the EMU countries, but they find no representation in the design of the ECB.

Perils of the national orientation

As we have seen, the ECB is the outcome of an institutional design adapted to national interests, a feature it shares with other EU institutions such as the Commission. This invites national conflicts in the public debate, as well as in the Governing Council. How important these conflicts become depends on the resolution of a question we raised in Chapter 1. Will monetary integration carry more or less divergence to the economies of the member states?

Even if these conflicts could be handled, we see long-run risks with the current arrangements. One comes from the considerable powers of the ECB, and the fact that political influence is confined to the appointment of its officers. The risk is that the appointments become a game of nationalistic politics and are not based upon competence for the task. To some degree, this will concern the appointment of governors for the NCBs. But a greater risk concerns the appointment to the Executive Board, particularly as these appointments can be vetoed by individual member states. We have already seen trouble on the one occasion such appointments have been made: witness the rift over Duisenberg vs. Trichet in the first appointment for President. Another example that shows the possible perils of a nationalistic approach is the stalemate in 1994 regarding the replacement of Jacques Delors as President of the Commission. Eventually that ended in the selection of a weak compromise candidate, Jaques Santer, who did not turn out to be very successful in this important position.

The other risk is a potential threat to long-run legitimacy. As long as the ECB maintains its considerable goal independence, it will be judged by its success in pursuing a policy that selects a specific short-run trade-off between inflation and output for

Europe as a whole. For instance, bad shocks or policy mistakes may lead to a severe European recession, and mounting unemployment may be blamed on the priorities set by the ECB. The ECB's legitimacy may suffer and hence its ability to act in a consistent way.

2.5 Possible reforms

The peculiar institutional design of the ECB is not a coincidence. It is a reflection of the common way the Union's member states tend to proceed with integration. On the one hand, most member states yearn for a bold 'European solution' in economic integration. On the other hand, they are very reluctant to give up national control. In the short run the ECB has responded to this dualistic design by choosing a particular form of communication about its policy and its decisions. In the longer run the result can be institutional dysfunction.

Long-run Treaty revisions

In the longer run, the path towards resolving these difficulties should involve a step mentioned already in the first MECB report (Begg et al., 1998), namely to radically redress the balance in the ECB's Governing Council in favour of the Executive Board. This could be achieved by introducing revolving terms for the NCB governors, along the lines of the 12-member US Open Market Committee, where no more than five (out of 12) Federal Reserve Bank presidents have voting rights.

Cutting the number of voting NCB governors would not in itself fully address the underlying problems. Appointments to the Executive Board would then become even more important. As long as they are made by the Council of Ministers, the nationalistic perspective remains and tension could mount with each yearly appointment. Some kind of quota system would be likely to develop, whereby candidates for the Board from countries not currently with a voting NCB governor would have greater chances of appointment.

To reduce the play of purely national interests, reforming the composition of the Governing Council should be combined with giving the European Parliament a much greater role in the appointment of the Executive Board. This would be beneficial for long-run legitimacy in that it would cut the long chains of delegation and give a voice in the appointment process to European interests cutting across national borders. The benefits in terms of higher legitimacy would be strengthened if the European Parliament itself was subject to an electoral reform fostering the building of cross-border coalitions and true European parties (see Dewatripont et al., 1995).

An important piece of reform to create a *European* Central Bank would be to remove the goal independence of the ECB. This would take some of the political heat out of the ECB's decisions, transferring its role to the more technical task of implementing a well-specified goal, preferably in the form of a European inflation target. But which body would specify the European inflation target? Under current EU design the most appealing possibility might be to apply the co-decision procedure.[10] As this procedure continues to give a strong weight to national interests, giving some or all of the agenda-setting rights to the European Parliament (after appropriate electoral reform) would be a better alternative.

Such reforms would require non-trivial changes in the Treaty. But reforms of the ECB structure may become a necessity, as more members are knocking on the door. A Governing Council with 25 or 30 members would be a nightmare that must be avoided. It is interesting to recall that German unification triggered a change in representation, cutting the number of Länder bank presidents represented on the Bundesbank Council from 16 to 9. The coming IGC has the explicit task of preparing the EU for enlargement. For the IGC to live up to this task, it must tackle a number of difficult issues, including voting rules in the Council of Ministers, the number of Commissioners, the size and role of the European Parliament (EP), etc. The Pandora's Box of comprehensive Treaty reform will thus be open, which constitutes a rare opportunity to discuss and pursue reforms of the ECB.

Short-run measures by the ECB itself

Awaiting such Treaty reform, the ECB must live within its current statutes. We have seen that these do not provide much help in enhancing the ECB's long-run legitimacy. To avoid the risk of faltering public trust, the ECB has to earn its legitimacy directly from the people of Europe. Issing (1999) has rightly argued that ultimately it will be the results that count. But just waiting for a long enough track record may be too risky or take too long.

In Section 2.3 we described how the ECB has, so far, decided to live within its statutes. One aspect where we sympathise with the present approach is the choice of collective accountability for the Governing Council's decisions. With the current composition of the Governing Council, the perception of the Council as a set of representatives of national interests is likely to remain. Publication of individual voting records and minutes focusing on individual differences may be counterproductive under these circumstances, but summary minutes not attributing individual

10. This means that: (i) the Commission proposes, (ii) the EP votes, (iii) after EP approval, the Council votes with qualified majority, in the opposite case an amended proposal is worked out by a Committee drawn from the EP and the Council of Ministers, which has to pass both bodies with a qualified majority.

views would be possible and helpful. We have indicated that the Council may find it easier and more effective to build a collective reputation, than relying on the combined individual reputations of its 17 members. A collective reputation may also give stronger enforcement down the line and may facilitate continuity through the gradual turnover of Council members.

This situation might change after institutional reforms like those described above. If the ECB becomes a goal-dependent central bank with its precise targets set elsewhere, the task of the Governing Council becomes less politically contentious. In this event individual accountability might become more palatable.

We find it much harder to agree with the *ex post* approach to transparency about policy. This approach makes it harder to predict actions by the ECB in the short to medium run, which might show up as unnecessary instability and risk premia in asset prices. It may make the ECB's reputation-building less effective. The approach also makes it harder to communicate directly with the public. As the indirect accountability through political representatives is missing, the ECB has to earn its legitimacy directly from the public. Educating the public about the intentions behind its policy thus becomes very important. But education does not easily take place through a smokescreen.

We have seen in Section 2.2 that ECB policy during the past year has been consistent with a variety of hypotheses regarding its policy behaviour, including the hypothesis that the development in some countries is given disproportionate weight. More precision about what the monetary policy strategy means would, therefore, seem to be in the ECB's own interest. This would involve mainly three changes.

First, the Council should publish its internal forecasts about euro-wide inflation, output (and money growth, as long as the reference values remain) – with appropriate qualifications with regard to forecast uncertainty. In the last few months there have been promising signs that the ECB is changing its attitude; the President has hinted at the possibility of internal forecasts eventually being published, perhaps as early as next year.

Second, the Council should continue in this direction by replacing the present mode of relatively vague *ex post* explanations of its policy moves by an explicit discussion, in writing and in speeches, of alternative contingency plans for policy. Alternative policy scenarios should be tied to the published forecasts so as to provide a clearer illustration of the Council's interpretation of its chosen policy framework. In short, the ECB should adopt the *ex ante* approach to transparency. Such an approach is likely to be more conducive to informing the markets of its way of making policy, as well as building trust in a European setting of many constituencies with a patchwork of experience in monetary policy.

Third, the two-pillar approach stands in the way of *ex ante* transparency. It is hard to interpret and leads to occasional conflicts of objectives. A single pillar, an inflation target, would help in that respect, without chipping away at the ECB's independence or credibility.

3

Financial stability

The creation of EMU is not only a matter of monetary policy. The framers of the Maastricht Treaty also had a vision of drastically transforming European financial markets and financial institutions. How adapted to this task are the existing institutions? Do they adequately promote financial stability? We use our current understanding of financial regulation to ask whether financial stability is preserved or jeopardised in today's, and tomorrow's, EMU. Our view is that systemic risks have already increased – and will increase further – and that the existing regulatory and supervisory framework is too narrow to cope with some of the emerging risks. The underlying problem is similar to that in monetary policy: a collision in institution design between the desire of European *economic* integration and the reluctance to give up national *political* control. For this reason, the centralised solution advocated by many observers appears unlikely in the short to medium run, and we discuss what can be done by the ECB under current institutions. Rather than improvised or institutionalized cooperation among national supervisory authorities, we advocate a number of measures in the direction of decentralised regulation.

3.1 Why do we need financial regulation?

Financial market failures

Financial regulation is required for three main reasons: to protect the consumer, to avoid the social cost of failure by financial institutions and to diminish systemic risk. The consumer needs protection because the quality of financial contracts is not directly observable. Failures of financial institutions have a social cost mainly because of contagion effects that arise when the soundness of the financial industry as a whole is open to doubt. Financial stability is a public good, and as such it is likely to be underprovided if left only to the markets.

To protect small and uninformed consumers is important in its own right. There is, however, a further reason to be concerned with financial stability. Crisis or bankruptcy in a certain bank occasionally triggers a run of depositors on an another bank with similar characteristics, as described in Box 3.1. This kind of contagion helps explain the severity of banking crises, including serious deflationary episodes such as the Great Depression. It is sometimes argued that in today's well developed financial systems, a bank confronted with a deposits flight should not have any problem in replacing those funds by a loan from the interbank market as long as it is solvent. This is not always the case because of interbank market imperfections of the kind that explain phenomena such as the 'ethnic bank crisis' in the UK (see

BOX 3.1   Banking Crises

The definition of systemic risk deserves clarification. The fundamental source of risk is that banks hold long-term assets to match their short-term liabilities. As a result, in the event of a bank run, when the depositors suddenly decide to withdraw a large fraction of their deposits, the bank needs to obtain funding through other channels but may be unable to do so fast enough to stay in operation. Two cases have to be distinguished:

- The institution may be solvent and illiquid;

- The institution may be insolvent and illiquid.

The first case is the one that justifies Bagehot's principles for lending in last resort. This mechanism is to be set in motion if it is feared that solvent institutions may be closed down simply because of the depositors' irrational herd behaviour. In the worst case, initially-solvent banks may become insolvent because they are forced to liquidate their assets at a fire-sale price in order to obtain liquidity.

The bulk of historical evidence (see among others Gorton, 1988) shows that the case for illiquid solvent institutions has been overstated, depositors rarely run without a cause, so that the large majority of runs affect banks with solvency problems. In fact, it is very difficult to determine whether an institution in financial distress is insolvent or illiquid. Quite often runs are triggered by wholesale depositors who may have accurate information. As for systemic effects, except for the case where the bank crisis combines with a currency crisis, a withdrawal in one bank tends to generate a new deposit in another one. Finally, by contrast with 19th century financial environment, developed countries have the benefit of having liquid interbank markets where institutions that are viewed as solvent can borrow from other institutions. The case of the illiquid solvent institution arises for those institutions perceived as insolvent by wholesale depositors and by the peer institutions from which they would otherwise borrow.

In practice, for banks facing financial distress, rescue is the rule and liquidation is the exception (Goodhart and Schoenmaker, 1995). In the US at the time of the Saving and Loans crisis, banks with very poor rating (a CAMEL rating of 5) were given the privilege of using the discount window to obtain funds. In addition, there is a clear consensus among regulators that some banks 'too-big-to-fail' cannot be allowed to generate systemic risk. So if some insolvent banks are rescued, is it because regulators are 'wet' or because they recognise strong enough externalities to resist market discipline and avoid liquidating insolvent financial institutions? That question has not yet been satisfactorily answered.

What are the costs of a banking crisis? Estimates differ widely. They depend on the business cycle as it affects the percentage of loans that have to be written off. The cost of Japan's banking crisis is estimated at 30% of GDP, that of the Mexico at 27% (*Financial Times*, 17 September 1998 and 2 October 1998 respectively). For the US, the S&L crisis resulted in the liquidation of 1600 thrifts and a total cost of 2% of GDP (Santomero and Hoffman, 1998), but those costs are 'multiplied by initial inaction and bureaucratic inefficiency'. The cost of the Swedish crisis has been estimated well over some 3.5% of GDP (Santomero and Hoffman, 1998).

Box 3.4 on page 54). More recently, the development of unsecured payment systems, interbank markets and OTC derivatives markets have created a new web of short-term exposures among banks and other financial institutions. This web provides new channels for contagion in the financial system.

A financial institution in distress may affect both the asset and liability sides of non-financial institutions' balance sheets. On the asset side, firms may suddenly be deprived of their credit lines, with serious disruptive effects until alternative lenders examine their creditworthiness. On the liability side, as the assets of a failing bank are frozen, depositors find that very liquid assets are rapidly being transformed into quite illiquid ones. The combination of these two externalities may have a depressing impact on economic activity, which may be hard to counteract with increased liquidity, since open market operations do not supply credit or liquidity directly to the agents in need. The importance of these market failures depends on the economic and financial environment and thus evolves over time. But adequate regulation can diminish their likelihood.

Regulatory safety nets

Prospective market failures have led regulators to supply a 'safety net' in financial markets. Most developed countries have introduced a *deposit insurance* system eliminating credit risk for small depositors. Deposit insurance provides consumer protection and drastically reduces one source of financial contagion: bank runs. All EU countries – and thus all members of EMU – are subject to the EU 1992 Deposit Guarantee Scheme Directive, which requires deposit insurance up to 20,000 ECU per deposit.

Other universal parts of the safety net are the *supervision of individual financial institutions* and the *monitoring of possible systemic risk*. Collecting adequate information allows regulators to take proper action should a crisis arise. Supervision and monitoring further induce financial institutions to develop their own systems of internal control. The different components of the safety net may be centralised within the central bank or in other institutions.

Without mechanisms to protect uninformed depositors, it may be optimal to systematically bail out banks in trouble. A deposit insurance mechanism, however, drastically reduces the social costs of banks' distress, which makes it much harder to justify the systematic bailout of banks. Recent banking crises – in the United States, Mexico and Japan – made taxpayers aware that in the end they will have to foot the bill. Efficiency points in the same direction. The familiar moral-hazard argument suggests that expectations of a bailout lead to excessively high risk-taking by financial institutions. Allowing institutions to go bankrupt may thus lead to higher efficiency by inducing more prudent lending and investment behaviour. A trade-off emerges between providing the right *ex ante* incentives for financial firms and avoiding the *ex post* social costs associated with realised failures.

This trade-off makes it difficulty to design a regulatory mechanism. Regulators have tended to overprotect bank claim holders at the expense of taxpayers. Kaufman (1999) argues forcefully that 'By delaying both the imposition of sanctions on troubled institutions and the resolution of economically insolvent institutions, bank regulators have often been poor agents both for their healthy, premium paying banks and for the taxpayers, who are the ultimate backstop for insurance funds.' Financial institutions facing the threat of bankruptcy in France and Japan have systematically been bailed out. The example of Japan's Long Term Credit Bank illustrates how, in some countries, the liquidation of a bank is a very remote possibility.

Two main problems emerge. First is the difficulty for the authorities to *commit* themselves to a hands-off policy: once a banking crisis is under way, refusing to intervene may carry substantial social costs – particularly in the case of large failures. The other problem is *regulatory capture*, which arises when stakeholders in troubled financial institutions may have considerably more political clout with the regulators than anonymous taxpayers.

3.2 Has EMU increased systemic risk?

While the macroeconomic difficulties of dealing with idiosyncratic shocks has been one of the main ingredients in the debate on the pros and cons of EMU membership, the risks for financial stability in individual countries have not attracted the attention they deserve. Whether local failures spill over on to financial firms elsewhere in EMU depends on future developments in European banking and financial industries. Systemic risk can be defined as the risk of an event which results in the 'impairing of the general well functioning (of an important part) of the financial system' (De Bandt and Hartmann, 1998). It is useful to distinguish two types of systemic risks. One is the risk for a disturbance large widespread enough for a number of financial institutions to get into trouble at the same time. The other is the risk that one or more failures spill over to other financial institutions in a domino-like fashion.

What is EMU's 'financial system'? A crisis in a small member country could be considered systemic or not, depending upon whether we take the perspective of the single country or the Union as a whole. Table 3.1 indicates the relative size of assets of each member state's credit institutions. Finland, Ireland and Portugal represent such small shares that even a major financial crisis in one of these countries would not be considered systemic for the entire Union. In the present less than fully financially

Table 3.1 Assets of European Credit Institutions to Euroland total (%)

Austria	3.47
Belgium	5.09
Germany	36.67
Spain	6.93
Finland	0.95
France	23.13
Ireland	1.02
Italy	12.11
Luxembourg	4.04
Netherlands	5.24
Portugal	1.33

Source: ECB

integrated EMU, we believe that a European perspective should still treat a crisis in one of the member countries as a serious event. However, given the limitations on the ECB's intervention procedures, this may be a minor point.

On the other hand, it might be argued that confining the discussion to Europe is too narrow. Many problems of financial stability are truly global in nature, as witnessed by the recent turmoil caused by crises in Asia and Latin America. Would it thus not be more productive to discuss global financial reform? We think not. First, the world is not on the same currency. European financial institutions are likely to develop disproportionately in the first few years of the euro. Second, most discussions of 'global financial architecture' come up with reform proposals that are badly lacking in realism, as they require supranational, global institutions. Discussing reform at the European level is more productive, as institutions capable of enforcement already exist or could at least be conceived.

We believe that the creation of EMU may contribute to higher systemic risk in European financial markets for several reasons: greater macroeconomic risks, more competition inducing greater risk-taking by banks and new channels of financial contagion.

Macroeconomic risks

In the pre-EMU stage European countries had some – albeit limited – room for manoeuvre in meeting domestic booms and busts by changing domestic interest rates. With a common monetary policy this possibility is gone. A pessimistic – but perhaps realistic – view is that national fiscal policy will be quite a poor substitute. In the absence of further economic integration, it is thus likely that we will see more variations in national economic conditions during the next decade.

Cycles tend to be accompanied by wide asset price swings. Crashing asset values – particularly for commercial property – following a previous boom dramatically raised the share of non-performing loans in the banks' portfolios and helped trigger the recent banking crises in Europe and elsewhere. For example, Table 3.2 shows the situation in the Nordic Countries at the time of the bank crisis. With real estate loans representing a third of bank assets, a fall of 40% in property prices – as these countries have witnessed – stood to erase more that 10% of asset value, a number in excess of non-performing loans.

Table 3.2 Nordic Banks at Crisis Time
Exposure to non-performing and real estate loans in 1992 (% of bank assets)

	Non performing loans	Real estate loans
Finland	7.7	n.a.
Norway	9.3	32.5
Sweden	8.3	35.1

Source: Eichengreen and Wyplosz (1993)

Profitability of banks

If financial integration in Europe is successful, it will mean more competition in financial markets and fiercer competition across national borders between existing and new banks – both on the lending and borrowing side – with lower current and future expected profits. The squeeze is expected to affect both sides of bank balance sheets.

On the asset side, European financial markets will become more like Anglo-Saxon financial markets as the private sector finances a larger share of its investments through marketable financial instruments. Impetus for disintermediation and expansion of the Euro market for corporate paper and bonds is provided by the emergence of very liquid markets for interbank and government securities and thus a single reference yield curve in euros at short as well as long maturities. This makes it possible to price corporate paper denominated in euros with reference to this common yield curve (in the same way as the previous spreads *vis-à-vis* LIBOR and PIBOR). As discussed in Chapter 1, the process has already taken off. Issues in the market for euro-denominated corporate bonds increased at a rate close to 200% in the past year. This, however, may just be the beginning. On the basis of the trends in the US markets for corporate bonds and papers in the last two decades, market financing could replace up to a third of the current lending from European banks to corporate customers (McCauley and White (1997)). Banks may certainly raise their fees and commissions as corporate bond issues expand, but the most likely effect is a squeeze on bank profitability, with diminishing volumes of borrowing and falling margins.

On the liability side, investment funds – providing liquid euro-denominated investments without exchange rate risk in bonds and equities – are going to suck up household savings previously going into bank deposits. Parts of these funds are no doubt going to be channelled through existing institutions, raising revenue through management fees. More importantly, large institutional investors like insurance companies and pension funds that have held their most liquid funds as relatively low yielding bank deposits, will shift to the euro repo and deposit markets.

Overall, from the viewpoint of financial stability, disintermediation might have some advantages. In particular, continuous market pricing of corporate risk will be available to a greater extent than before – something that will allow banks to better assess the riskiness of bank portfolios. Yet even if some new business opportunities for existing banks arise, the net result for most of them, *ceteris paribus*, is likely to be a squeeze on profit margins through a higher cost of funds as well as a lower expected return on investments. This in turn implies a lower opportunity cost of bankruptcy and more risk taking (as banks trade off their need for increased profitability against the opportunity cost of going bankrupt).

Mergers, acquisitions and transnational banking

Existing banks are likely to take further, more drastic steps when their future profitability is threatened. A process of concentration has already begun with the purpose of creating institutions large enough to successfully compete in the future European arena. While the process has so far mostly taken place within countries, aiming at producing national champions first, many observers expect the next step to be the creation of large European *transnational* banks. One path towards such institutions is the opening of bank branches in other European countries, an activity that has been going on for some years. So far, however, the activities of these branches remain modest. Some cross-border alliances have indeed formed, particularly involving Scandinavian banks, including the merger creating Merita-Nordbanken (a Finnish-Swedish alliance) and the purchase by Swedish SEB of BfG, Germany's fifth-largest privately owned bank. Dexia, created from the merger of France's CLF and Belgium's CCB, has emerged as a leader in lending to local and regional governments. Boundaries between banks, insurance companies, investment banks and securities dealers are also becoming increasingly blurred as financial conglomerates emerge. Recent examples of bank–insurer mergers include Fortis-Generale Banque, ING-BBL, SE Banken-Trygg Hansa, CS-Winterthur and INA-Banco di Napoli.

What does this evolution imply for financial stability? No clear conclusion emerges. One view is that following the creation of a monetary union and the concomitant moves towards larger transnational banks and financial conglomerates, financial firms are likely to diversify both their assets and their liabilities. This should improve individual risk-return trade-offs and financial stability in general. Another view is that this effect will not materialise any time soon because banks will remain 'home-biased'. This view assumes that a strong informational advantage will continue to provide local banks with a competitive edge in dealing with local borrowers.

Interbank exposures and contagion

Up to this point we have discussed whether the creation of the monetary union might endanger financial stability by increasing the likelihood of bank failures, either by raising macroeconomic risks or by lowering expected profits and hence inviting greater risk taking by banks. On top of the greater risks of bank failures, however, the reshaping of European financial markets might raise systemic risk by creating new channels for financial contagion.

Of particular importance are the large short-run exposures that arise among banks and other financial institutions in connection with their trading and settlements in the markets for currency, short-term loans and deposits and derivative instruments. These interbank transactions give rise to asset positions that are often large, uncollateralized and concentrated in a few institutions. Even though these positions have a very short duration – no more than days for lending in overnight markets or settlements in currency markets, and no more than hours in payment systems – they can be the source of major problems. They can transmit problems from a failing institution to others. In addition large interbank exposures can create uncertainty about the size and location of problems at crisis time.

EMU is affecting European interbank exposures in a number of ways, mostly with favourable effects.

- Intra-European currency trade, and hence the exposures arising in the settlements of this trade, is eliminated.

- Intra-European payments were previously often made through arrangements between correspondent banks, which meant large and uncollateralized exposures for two to three days.

- Large payments in euros between member countries are rapidly migrating into TARGET or EBA. (See Begg et al. (1998) for a discussion of TARGET.) TARGET, the payment system run by the central banks, demands collateral even for intra-day credit, which means much lower exposures and lower risk of contagion. The large use of EBA, a private payment system, could have been an additional source of systemic risk, as pointed out by Danthine et al. (1999, p.91). Fortunately, this risk seems limited. As EBA imposes both a limit on settlements and makes certain demands of collateral, the effect of a bank's failure on its counterparts is limited. Moreover, larger payments are systematically channelled through TARGET, while EBA and other private payment systems are used for smaller-value transactions.

Successful financial integration in Europe, however, will greatly expand other types of interbank exposures. As discussed in Chapter 1, an integrated interbank market for short-term money has already emerged. Expanding deposit and OTC derivative markets in euros, and the trade in euros vs. other currencies, will raise the uncollateralized exposures against other European banks. Furthermore, the ongoing concentration and diversification of European financial institutions are creating larger financial actors who are active in many interbank markets and becoming counterparts to many other institutions. Concentration thus goes hand in hand with higher exposures and higher systemic risk. Furthermore, tendencies towards transnational banking will make the ripples of a failure more directly felt in different parts of Europe.

Interbank exposure presents a particular problem for monitoring and supervision. The size of banks' exposure is not adequately captured by their balance sheets. For instance, settlement risks do not appear at all. There is also no reporting of the total exposure, across different markets, *vis-à-vis* other actors – which is the relevant measure from the perspective of contagion. Furthermore, data is typically made available at the end of the reporting period. As exposures can shift quickly over a few days, this is clearly inadequate. In fact, little is known about the distribution of interbank exposures across banks and time (Furfine, 1999). The lack of information may not be confined to regulators and other outside observers; many banks may not have internal systems that allow them to adequately measure their total exposure towards other financial institutions at a given point in time.

Summary conclusions

The overall trend points clearly towards more competition among financial institutions in Europe, and towards a larger interbank exposure because of more extensive European interbank operations. Furthermore, this development occurs in a European context where substantial transnational banking is just around the corner and where local macroeconomic shocks can no longer be met through monetary policy. How to cope with systemic risk is thus quickly becoming a burning issue at the level of the Eurosystem.

3.3 The present distribution of supervisory power

Concern about financial stability in EMU has been rising recently. The common view is that combining centralised monetary policy with decentralised regulation and supervision is an inconsistent arrangement. Some of the criticisms are well founded; others lack a serious foundation. Before dealing with the main issues we briefly refute a couple of ill-founded criticisms.

Ill-founded criticisms

There is nothing wrong with the separation of monetary and regulatory power. It is true that a central bank responsible for financial regulation has the advantage of coordinating in-house monetary and regulatory policies. Regulatory powers also allow the central bank easy access to relevant information on individual financial institutions for playing its traditional role of lender of last resort (LOLR). But centralisation has its drawbacks: a central bank in charge of monetary and regulatory functions might face conflicting objectives. In particular, the conduct of monetary policy may become more lenient in fighting inflation if higher interest rates jeopardise banks' solvency.

Looking across European countries, current arrangements vary a great deal, as Table 3.3 illustrates. In about half of the countries the central bank is in charge of banking supervision, but no central bank is in charge of all financial regulation. The international trend seems to be towards a separation of the two functions, which according to some observers (Di Noia and Giorgio, 1999) will reinforce the efficiency of financial institutions.

A second ill-founded criticism is that the Eurosystem does not provide financial stability because the ECB cannot provide

Table 3.3   Regulatory arrangements across countries

	Banking	Securities	Insurance
Europe 15			
Austria	G	G	G
Belgium	BS	BS	I
Germany	B	S	I
Denmark	U	U	U
Spain	CB	S	I
Finland	BS	BS	I
France	B/CB	S	I
Greece	CB	S	I
Ireland	CB	CB	G
Italy	CB	S	I
Luxembourg	BS	BS	I
Netherland	CB	S	I
Portugal	CB	S	I
Sweden	U	U	U
UK	U	U	U
U.S.	CB	S	I
Japan	U	U	U

U = Universal Regulator (as the FSA in the UK or Japan)
CB = Central Bank
B, S, I are specialized regulatory agencies for the banking, securities and insurance industries respectively.
BS = Regulator in charge of both banking and securities industries.
G = Government Agency

Source: Adapted from Lannoo (1999)

ender-of-last-resort support to financial institutions facing financial distress. This is incorrect because lender-of-last-resort support to financial institutions exists in the hands of the 11 Treasuries. One of the main lessons of recent banking crises is that the bailout of banks is ultimately a fiscal policy issue (see, among others, Calomiris, 1999). At the current stage of European integration, when fiscal policy remains in the hands of member states, it is hardly realistic to delegate this responsibility to the ECB. It is also incorrect because it has never been established that lender-of-last-resort support was good – some view it as reducing market discipline. Moral hazard problems seriously undermine the arguments for the policy of systematic bailouts that has so far prevailed in continental Europe. Recent examples include Banco di Napoli in Italy, Banesto in Spain and Crédit Lyonnais in France. More general is the example of France where no bank has ever been liquidated. From that point of view, creation of a monetary union with a new distribution of roles may be a golden opportunity to further enhance market discipline by making the present safety net more transparent.

The real issues in the assessment of the financial stability in the euro zone are two-fold. Do existing mechanisms guarantee the necessary amount of coordination to deal with financial crises? And do they give the right incentives to respond efficiently in the event of a crisis? We will examine these questions at three different – but related – levels. First, we look at the procedures for the rescue or liquidation of financial institutions in the event of a large domestic banking crisis. Next, we ask what mechanisms are in place to handle a crisis involving a transnational financial institution. Finally, we address systemic risk issues. As we proceed in this hierarchy, the responsibility of the ECB becomes more important.

Large domestic bank crises

If a crisis is confined to a national bank, the relevant member state's national central bank may decide to rescue the institution, presumably in cooperation with the supervisory authority (if different from the central bank) and the Treasury, as discussed in Box 3.2. To meet our definition of a purely domestic crisis it is essential that the crisis with a domestic bank affects neither the ECB nor other NCBs. As long as each member state retains the responsibility for regulation, the costs of regulatory failure involving domestic financial institutions should remain strictly at the national level. Under these conditions the incentives are right and very limited cooperation between the NCB and the ECB is required as long as NCBs have permanent access to liquidity from the ECB.

In principle, therefore, a large domestic banking crisis can be met by a speedy response at no cost for the ECB. As previously discussed, there may be a potential danger of collusion between

BOX 3.2   Domestic bank rescue operations in Euroland

A bank rescue can be structured in different ways. A distressed bank requires an emergency cash injection, or additional capital, frequently both. As a bank in crisis is not able to obtain funds in the interbank market, it depends on intervention by the Treasury or the national central bank, either through a direct intervention or as facilitator in arranging a private solution. Because central bank profits accrue to Treasuries, the burden of the costs is always borne by the taxpayers.

1. The first-best solution is that the authority in charge – usually the regulatory agency in charge of supervision – finds a group of investors willing to buy out the bank at no cost to the taxpayers, as in the recent LTCM crisis in the US. This 'life-boat' solution requires coordination of potential private investors who can take over the defaulting bank. If the market for take-overs was efficient, this coordination would not be required and the market mechanism would solve the bank crisis. For example, creditors of the bank who know that their assets are at risk have the right incentives to avoid a default. Still, a cooperation mechanism is required because each creditor by itself would be better off by free riding on the others.

2. Another solution implies nationalizing the bank, accompanied by a Treasury announcement that the bank's liabilities will be fully guaranteed, as was the case in the Scandinavian banking crisis. The short term cash injection problem is solved at taxpayers expense, but additional funds have to be raised in the market in order to replace the bank's depleted capital. This responsibility falls on the central bank or the Treasury. The funds can be raised in the money market, either by selling government securities or by borrowing against collateral.

3. The ECB cannot stay idle, though, and the choice is unpalatable. It may adopt an accommodating stance to avoid a liquidity shortage, but monetary aggregates then increase, which may conflict with its fundamental objective. Ideally, it would relax its policy temporarily and mop up excessive liquidities at a latter stage.

4. Because of its exceptional character, the losses generated by the bank rescue will not be automatically passed on to the other NCBs. Still, it seems technically possible that *ex post* the ECB may declare that the operation is in the common interest of financial stability in the euro area. If so, the losses will be shared among the Eurosystem participants.

Because no bank crisis has developed since the beginning of EMU, it is difficult to know whether the sharing of losses by all the NCBs is just a theoretical possibility or whether it will be routinely applied.

the bank in trouble and its NCB (or the supervisory authority). But this danger has not become greater due to the creation of EMU, as the cost of regulatory capture is still borne by the taxpayers in the member state.

A serious potential difficulty concerns the incentives for information transmission between the NCBs and the ECB when trying to solve a financial crisis. There is no conflict of interests as long as the ECB does not bear the cost of financial distress. The ECB has no reason not to inform an NCB of any abnormal operation taking place either in the European payment system or interbank market. Conversely, an NCB holding information about domestic banks in trouble has nothing to gain from withholding this information from the ECB.

Unfortunately, the current rules of the Eurosystem make it unclear whether the full cost of an intervention deemed exceptional will be entirely borne at the national level. This is a critical condition in our assessment. Yet Article 32.4 of the ESCB Statutes states:

The Governing Council may decide that national central banks shall be indemnified against costs incurred in connection with the issue of banknotes or in exceptional circumstances for specific losses arising from monetary policy operations undertaken for the ESCB. Indemnification shall be in a form deemed appropriate in the judgement of the Governing Council; these amounts may be offset against the national central banks' monetary income.

There could be some ambiguity in the interpretation of this point. At present, the official view seems to be that it excludes the financing of national bank distress. How it will actually play out after a crisis remains to be seen.

In need of clarification

The mechanism in place, in principle, leaves the full responsibility of the bailout or liquidation decision in the hands of the NCBs. Two aspects of this mechanism need clarification.

- A very large rescue operation may require some degree of coordination in the channelling of funds to the NCB or the Treasury that needs them. In addition, a large rescue may affect the amount of liquidity available in the market and thus influence the monetary policy of the ECB. How the ECB will react to a liquidity shortage caused by a crisis is important for systemic risk.

- Article 35.4 of its Statutes allows the ESCB to decide after a crisis to share the costs of a bailout operation among the NCBs, if it is judged to concern overall financial stability. If this happens – or is expected to happen – it would radically change incentives for the NCBs and the ECB discussed above. If cost sharing is ruled out – which must be stated unambiguously *ex ante* – some NCB or Treasury may be unable or unwilling to intervene, which could imperil financial stability. This is a high-stake issue with no easy way out, yet the ECB has so far remained completely silent.

Transnational bank crises

If, as we expect, continued pressure from competition in banking and from disintermediation leads to the emergence of large transnational financial institutions, a new form of crisis becomes a real possibility. This will be a standard public-good financing problem. Although each country where the bank operates might reap some benefits from a bailout of the institution, none will be willing to contribute the full amount required. As a consequence, liquidation of transnational banks will be more frequent than their bailout. This may be good news if we believe that there has been an excessive tendency to bail out institutions in continental Europe, leading to a strengthening of market discipline and a reduction of moral hazard. But it could as well result in bank liquidations that have potentially high social costs due to contagion in the financial system.

The orderly bailout or liquidation of transnational banks therefore becomes an important challenge for regulatory institutions, as recognised by the European Commission (Box 3.3). The institutional response has been an attempt to create new means of cooperation. Some of the response has been reactive. Thus, each of the cross-border bank mergers discussed earlier has triggered new bilateral *ad hoc* cooperation between the corresponding regulatory authorities. At a more general level the European Commission's so-called BCCI directive has removed the legal obstacles to the diffusion of confidential information and has enabled regulators to exchange privileged information. In a more proactive mode, the Banking Supervision Committee as well as the Groupe de Contact have become mechanisms for more extensive cooperation. The Banking Supervision Committee in the ECB is composed of representatives of the banking supervisory authorities of the EU countries. It is developing into a key forum for multilateral cooperation in Europe. As a more informal structure, the Groupe de Contact has discussed individual banking cases from a multilateral perspective (Padoa-Schioppa, 1999).

It is reassuring that channels for coordination among different regulatory authorities do exist. Still, the supervisory task goes beyond information gathering. In the case of a major transnational crisis the requirements for swift and decisive action could be very demanding. The usual deadline to act is the opening of the market on the next business day. Without pre-established clear-cut rules and a well established chain of command, it is far from evident that effective cooperation of regulators could be forthcoming in real time.

Our concerns are informed by well known pitfalls in relying on mere cooperation among regulators, in contrast with centralised regulation. One problem is the possibility of

---

BOX 3.3   The European Commission view on regulatory cooperation

'The Commission would see great merit in developing 'ad hoc' and streamlined arrangements for close coordination between front-line authorities. Such an arrangement could draw from the membership of existing structures. In this way, it would avoid the duplication and proliferation of structures (e.g. Groupe de Contact, FESCO and Conference of Insurance Supervisors and their parent committees, BAC, HLSS and IC).'

'EU legislation provides a legally binding underpinning for cross-border co-operation between banking supervisors. These rules are managed through bilateral Memoranda of Understanding between national supervisors. Recently, some have argued that these arrangements are no longer sufficiently robust to contain cross-border effects of failure of large institutions. The Commission does not subscribe to the view that present arrangements are unsuitable for the present state of the single banking market. However it considers that there is a need for high-level political assessment, encompassing all national and EU level institutions with an interest in banking supervision, of the condition under which a review of present arrangements for banking supervision could be required.'

Excerpts from 'Financial Services: implementing the framework for financial markets: Action Plan.' Communication of the Commission (1999, p.14)

regulatory *competition*: each country may find it tempting to opt for a lower level of regulation than others, in the hope of attracting more banking business, enhancing the profitability of the country's financial institutions. The result is an insufficient level of regulation in each country. Another problem concerns the phenomenon of *regulatory capture* presented at the outset of this chapter. The point here is that the risk of collusion between the regulator and the regulated institutions may increase in the wake of coordination between regulators from different countries. Suppose that a truthful report from the domestic regulator to their European counterparts may harm an influential domestic financial institution. The domestic regulator may then have incentives to delay its report and even to minimise the risk of a bank crisis, at least until reaching its own decision that the closure of the bank is inevitable.[1] Furthermore, the incentives to delay the bankruptcy of a financial institution may be higher if the country in charge of regulation does not pay the full cost of bankruptcy if there is a cost-sharing arrangement among the different NCBs.

What are the possible ways of dealing with the costs of the rescue operation affecting transnational financial institutions? In order to avoid bruising negotiations at the time of crisis, a binding rule must be agreed upon *ex ante*. The most likely solution will be to collect resources from member governments according to a set key. The logic is that the rescue of transnational banks calls for transnational funding. There are, however, problems. First, who will set the amount of the rescue? In the absence of a binding ceiling, moral hazard could be serious, leading to controversies and transaction costs possibly high enough to scuttle any rescue operation. Second, what would be the key? A simple solution would seem to be to adopt the key designed to share revenues in the ESCB, but Luxembourg's share, for instance, will seem unrelated to its relative size in banking (Table 3.1, page 43), which makes this approach more complicated to set in motion. This feature attenuates the moral hazard problem but may prevent swift reaction. Clearly, in the absence of some central institution, rescues will be problematic, and the setting up of such an institution is controversial.

We return to this question in Section 3.4.

Dealing with systemic risk

A truly systemic risk would occur at the European level in the presence of a liquidity crisis or the failure of a major financial institution with a major risk of spill-over. This would surely be a

---

1. A possible counter argument is due to Laffont and Martimort (1998) who argue that concentration of information to a single regulator will generally worsen the problem of regulatory capture.

situation where the ECB should take the lead. One mechanism that the ECB could use would be a large injection of liquidity against collateral. Since a systemic crisis typically reduces inflation pressure – even if its epicentre is in an EMU-peripheral country – it would probably not be a very controversial decision to carry out such an injection.

A large injection of liquidity, however, may not be enough. It is not clear that open market (repo) operations alone constitute an effective instrument when dealing with a systemic crisis. Will the banks that receive these funds channel them in the most efficient way? The experience of the UK in the aftermath of the BCCI crisis (Box 3.4) should be seen as a warning: deposits were withdrawn from small banks supposed to be solvent, while the larger institutions receiving the deposits did not channel the funds back to the small banks. In the end, only the intervention of the Bank of England allowed for a safe landing.

A large monetary injection by the ECB may provide some stabilization in the context of a systemic crisis, but the

---

BOX 3.4   The BCCI affair

On 5 July 1991, the Bank of Credit and Commerce International and its subsidiaries in more than 60 countries around the world were closed down. The biggest bank fraud in history had just come to an end. Two lessons can be drawn from the BCCI crisis: first it takes time and effort for regulators to gather all the information that is internationally disseminated; second, the closure of a bank may have unfortunate consequences for other similar banks.

1. The nature of BCCI operations, funding of known terrorist and laundering of drug money (mainly in the Tampa branch in Florida) first escaped the regulators. The most accurate expression to describe the BCCI activities is that of 'a bank within a bank'. The shell bank was transparent to the supervisory authority (The Bank of England) but had nothing to do with the real activities of the inside bank that was taking deposits unrecorded in the accounts prepared for the regulators. The Bank of England did have information on BCCI irregularities since October 1990, but it considered that regulatory action taken under the then-prevalent legislation on the basis of available evidence would have allowed to prove 'bad banking', 'false and deceitful transactions' and 'inappropriate transactions', but not fraud. The international structure of the BCCI group allowed it to escape overall international supervision because some subsidiaries based in the Cayman Islands and in Luxembourg were protected by bank secrecy laws and were thus opaque to foreign regulators. The Luxembourg authorities admitted their inability to effectively supervise the bank's subsidiary and repeatedly requested the subsidiary to switch incorporation to another country. Globally, the BBCI affair shows how difficult Cupertino among regulators is. It was only after the Price Waterhouse audit of June 1991, which provided detailed evidence of widespread fraud, that the Bank of England was able to take action.

2. Even though BCCI activities were patently fraudulent, its demise triggered the so-called 'ethnic banks crisis' in the UK. The losses endured by depositors under the low deposit insurance protection (the deposit insurance scheme prevailing at that time insured 75% of deposits up to £20,000 for households and up to £48,000 for businesses) provoked a flight to quality, as depositors and in particular large depositors and municipalities withdrew their deposits from small banking institutions (including some building societies) and redeposited them into larger, presumably safer banks. The effect was a shortage of liquidity in the small banks and an excess of liquidity in the large ones. There was no lending through the interbank market to compensate for the depositors' movements. The Bank of England had to intervene by lending to the small financial institutions.

Reference: Max Hall, 'The BCCI affair', *Banking World*, September 1993 effectiveness of this mechanism will be severely hampered by the lags in the effects of monetary policy. Indeed, the crisis could spread much faster than the effects of the monetary policy. Evidence from the October 1987 crisis suggests that it was not the decision to expand monetary policy that prevented a wider crisis. More important was the Federal Reserve's urging money centre banks to maintain and to expand loans to their creditworthy brokerage firm customers (Brimmer, 1989). The same kind of market participants' coordination took place when the New York branch of the Fed intervened to help coordinate the resolution of the LTCM crisis in the fall of 1998.

Finally, a related problem concerns the list of admissible collateral. In the event of a crisis the value and credit rating of collateral may be reduced. If the ECB lacks sufficient information it may be reluctant to lend against collateral that has been downgraded by the market.

The perils of improvised cooperation

From a technical point of view, it is true that a crisis will not affect the Eurosystem because 'The Euro area central banker has neither the direct responsibility for supervising banks nor for bank stability' (Padoa-Schioppa, 1999, p.9). This is why, Danthine et al. (1999, p.92) say that 'The ECB is in this respect, a very different institution from the Fed – more concerned and more constrained [than the Fed] about the risks it may take on its own books'. Still, financial stability is the explicit responsibility of the ESCB (Article 3), and the euro area central banker 'has a vital interest in a stable and efficient banking industry...' (Padoa-Schioppa, 1999)

In our view, the ECB may have the right instruments to channel liquidity but it may not have the right tools for coping with major crises that involve more than one country. We do not question the fact that 'there are neither legal-cum-institutional, nor organizational, nor intellectual impediments to acting when needed' (Padoa-Schioppa, 1999). Neither do we question the willingness among regulators to cooperate. But preserving financial stability is also a matter of reacting swiftly and decisively. The lack of a formal structure for intervention is therefore worrisome.

Concerned with this very point, Padoa-Schioppa argues that the lack of transparency on 'the procedural and practical details of emergency action' (op cit. p.12) is in line with the idea of 'constructive ambiguity' that will limit moral hazard by making discretionary the access to central bank support. It is one thing to state that the support of the central bank is not a right and will only be obtained with some probability, but this is certainly not equivalent to stating that procedural arrangements to solve financial crises will be organised on a case-by-case basis. The difference is the swiftness with which the rescue or liquidation operation will be organized. It is true that the appropriate action may differ from one crisis to another. The October 1987 stock market crash required central bank intervention to avoid the total collapse of the market. The Barings crisis required, instead, intervention by the supervisory agency to achieve an orderly liquidation and the purchase of the institution by another bank. In both these cases the institution in charge was clearly identified and was able to act quickly. This is not the case within the current regulatory structure of EMU.

The existing institutional set-up relies too much on improvised cooperation in the event of a crisis of European dimensions. An analogy with military crises is appropriate in that these also require swift, decisive action. The failure of improvised attempts at cooperation among European nations to produce an adequate response to the crises in the former Yugoslavia should serve as a warning. It is not clear that putting together an effective multilateral response to a complex financial crisis is any easier than putting together an effective multilateral military response. A 'Kosovo approach' to financial stability is not good enough.

Summary

The Eurosystem seems to have the necessary mechanisms in place to preserve financial stability by decentralising responsibility to the member countries in case of a large domestic bank crisis (with some provisos previously mentioned). But it seems to lack well-defined mechanisms to cope with transnational bank crises or serious systemic risk. In particular, it is far from certain that cooperation between national authorities will be sufficiently swift.

To deal with these problems, we see two roads ahead. One is towards more centralisation, complementing the ECB with a European institution entrusted with supervisory and regulatory powers. This approach is becoming the conventional wisdom. The alternative is to move towards decentralisation, relying on full disclosure and market monitoring.

3.4 Possible reforms

Centralisation: economically sound, politically hopeless

Regulatory institutions in Europe have traditionally played an active role in the financial sector. This tradition may have contributed to the strong case that has been made for creating a centralised body within EMU for supervision and (perhaps) regulation (Begg et al., 1998; Lannoo, 1999). A logical counterpart to the ECB, such a body would collect supervisory information, act as an interlocutor independent from any national central bank and would provide reliable information both on individual institutions and on financial markets. A well functioning supranational body could overcome the problems of coordination mentioned above by solving a financial crisis directly at headquarters.

While attractive from the economic angle, such a solution is probably politically and administratively impossible at this stage. The problem is really the same as the problem with the design of the ECB: a collision between the desire for further economic integration and the unwillingness to give up national political control. Creating a centralised supervisory body would deprive national central banks or national regulatory bodies of their main remaining function, and is probably a step too far.

In addition, swift action requires the commitment of adequate resources or at least the clear identification that resources will be available when and if needed. In a national setting, the supervisory body is an agent of the national authorities and it is well understood that the taxpayer is in effect the lender of last resort. For a supranational body to be able to take swift action, it would be necessary to have a similar understanding. Given the costs of banking crises, potentially several times the budget of the European Union, centralisation is clearly not on the negotiating table.

A further obstacle is that the creation of a new supervisory body would almost surely require a Treaty revision. Article 105(6) of the Treaty allows for some centralisation of supervisory power: 'the ECB may perform specific tasks concerning policies relating to the prudential supervision of credit institutions and other financial institutions with the exception of insurance undertakings' (Statutes Chapter V, Article 25). But it does not really allow for the creation of an independent European regulatory body that would necessarily imply the transfer of some national power to the European level. Even if the member governments were willing to contemplate such a step and succeeded in hammering out an agreement, it is easy to foresee how politically difficult its ratification would be.

Decentralisation: the other economically sound approach

Accepting Europe's ambivalence towards its own future, we can ask what can be done under the current institutional arrangements. Fostering better cooperation among NCBs and national supervisory bodies is one way, apparently the implicitly chosen way. Fearful of the Kosovo syndrome, we explore alternative approaches. The idea here is to accept that supervision and regulation will remain decentralised for the foreseeable future and, indeed, to bring this set-up to its logical end, compensating institutional weaknesses (as previously outlined) with decentralised market solutions.

This approach should combine several elements. One would be to limit the risk of individual failures by providing better incentives for market participants and improving the information available to supervisors, including the ECB. Another element would be to complement the official lender-of-last-resort function with a market mechanism that could cope with shortages of liquidity. Finally, the reform should aim at limiting the contagious effects of financial institution failures.

Disclosure

The private sector (banks, depositors, borrowers) has the right incentives: no one wants to deal with an unsecured financial institution. The usual difficulty is that not enough is known about the health of financial institutions. This problem, known as information asymmetry, can be alleviated if financial institutions are required to truthfully reveal all the elements needed to pass judgement on their safety. Individual firms and households may not have the means of monitoring financial institutions, but banks can and are eager to know with whom they are dealing. This is also the task of market analysts and rating agencies. Thus, if the appropriate information is released, the private sector is likely to monitor financial institutions as closely as supervizing agencies currently do. This view forms the basis of the decentralised solution.

It might be wondered, however, whether the private sector would be as diligent and accurate as existing supervising agencies. These doubts ought to confront the experience of New Zealand where in 1996 a new regime of banking supervision was introduced. This is more fully described in Box 3.5. This new regime is designed to put the main responsibility for prudent risk management with the banks themselves and their directors, rather than with their supervisors. A cornerstone of the regime is to require each registered bank to make a quarterly disclosure statement on the health of the bank that goes much further than traditional audits of income statements and balance sheets. Banks are also required to publicly disclose their capital adequacy (including off balance sheet items), sectoral exposures, exposures to market risk, exposures to related parties, and – most importantly from the viewpoint of systemic risk – the number of large exposures, including interbank exposures, against individual counterparties. Moreover, the statement is to include not only end-of quarter exposures, but also peak exposures during the quarter.

Applied to EMU, such disclosure rules would greatly enhance available information to private market participants and supply the ECB with better information on the extent of systemic risk. Relative to current supervisory rules, it would improve the information of national supervisors. It would also increase information in the markets about the riskiness of individual banks. To make the disclosures, many banks would have to reform their internal systems for risk assessments and, by signing the disclosure statements guaranteeing the institution's health and compliance with the regulation, bank directors would have stronger incentives to take responsibility for prudent management.

We are certainly not advocating transposing the New Zealand regime wholesale to Europe. For one, New Zealand does not have deposit insurance. Suppressing deposit insurance in Europe would repeal the 1992 Deposit Insurance Directive, which might not be politically feasible. In the presence of deposit insurance, small depositors would lack the right incentives to act upon disclosed information and withdraw from banks they consider too risky. This would certainly eliminate one of the channels for market discipline. But there are other important channels for market discipline, especially the willingness of other financial institutions to accept exposures in the interbank market. The disclosure would have to be carefully designed, however, so as not to raise the probability of market failure in the wake of systemic shocks (see Cordella and Yeyati (1998)). In addition, it is important to bear in mind that the commitment to a no-bailout regime, which reduces moral hazard, is credible when banks are foreign owned, as is virtually the case in New Zealand. Interestingly, however, the EMU might approach this situation, as transnational banking becomes more prevalent.

BOX 3.5　The New Zealand experience with market discipline

In 1996, after extensive consultations with representatives of the banking industry, New Zealand implemented an original regulatory framework[1] which relied heavily on market mechanisms and market discipline. The scheme builds upon five complementary mechanisms:

1. Banks are required to have high accounting and independent auditing standards;

2. Depositors and investors in a bank have full access to information on the risks they are taking;

3. A system of fines and penalties creates incentives for bank managers not to take excessive risks or misrepresent relevant information;

4. There is no 'safety net', and, in particular, no deposit insurance, which creates incentives for bank customers to exert caution;

5. A specific procedure allows for the orderly closure of banks that are in financial distress: the regulator has the right to place registered banks under statutory management and appoint a manager with large powers.

This structure is designed to limit moral hazard and to allow the supervisor to devote less effort in monitoring the viability of individual banks and to concentrate instead on systemic events.

This regulatory framework does not rely on taxpayers money in order to rescue banks. This feature was a political necessity in New Zealand where the banking system is dominated by foreign banks and immediately reminds us of the EU case where pan-European banks are likely to be seen by taxpayers as 'foreign.'

continued

1. For a very informative description of the New-Zealand system, see D. G. Mayes, 'A Market Based Approach to Maintaining Systemic Stability: Experiences from New Zealand', Bank of Finland Discussion Paper 18/97

Box 3.5 continued

Disclosure and incentives to truthful reporting

In their quarterly statements, registered banks have to provide all the information that is deemed relevant for depositors and other bank customer who choose where to bank, as well as for financial markets which need to assess the soundness of banks' strategies. The bank directors are required to certify that the bank has an adequate procedure to monitor and control risks. False declarations are heavily punished and include unlimited personal civil liability for losses to the bank's creditors. Penalties for trying to cover up and get through a difficulty are greater than those from truthfully disclosing a loss or an excessive level of risk. This provides the incentives for directors to be well informed and also to reveal truthfully the banks' risk positions. The existence of independent directors plays an important role because they do not have conflicts of interest and are likely to provide more objective scrutiny. The disclosure statements are published in two forms. The abridged one, intended for depositors and bank customers, contains the main figures on the bank credit rating, capital ratios and information on peak exposure concentration. The complete statement contains the full information on the above items and is aimed at the professional analysts. The additional cost for the banks to issue detailed statements is not very high. Detailed statements had to be prepared anyway under the previous regulation, even if this was private information supplied to the Reserve Bank .

The dislosure statement should include information on:

■ directors and their interests;

■ the income statement and balance sheet;

■ asset quality and provisioning;

■ the number of large exposures (including interbank exposures), relative to bank equity – end of period as well as peaks during the period;

■ exposures to related parties, relative to tier 1 capital;

■ sectoral exposures;

■ capital adequacy, including off-balance-sheet items;

■ exposures to market risk (interest rates and exchange rates);

■ credit rating.

Orderly closure procedures

Consistent with the absence of deposit insurance, there is no implicit guarantee for registered banks. A procedure for the swift replacement of the bank's management is designed to let banks fail while minimizing the consequences for the banking system. Following the Reserve Bank recommendation, the Minister of Finance may place the bank under statutory management. This recommendation is issued when there is suspicion that the bank is insolvent, when the capital ratio falls below the prudential threshold, or when the bank refuses to consult and comply with a directive or behaves in a manner that generates difficulties to its partners or to the financial system. Placing an institution under statutory management is a way to limit forbearance and thus to 'gamble for resurrection'.

There seems to exist a high degree of public confidence in the stability of the financial system. It is not yet clear, however, whether this is the result of strict supervision rules or a consequence of the fact that most banks are foreign-owned and supervised in their home countries (and New Zealand's success would be due to free riding on foreign supervisory authorities). In any event, transposing wholesale the New Zealand scheme to Europe would not only be simplistic, it would also be dangerous. It seems difficult or impossible to switch to no deposit insurance in Europe, and absent deposit insurance depositors would lack the right incentives to withdraw from the banks they consider too risky. Another difficulty is that full disclosure needs to be carefully designed in order not to reveal a bank's strategy to its competitors.

Proposals of a New Zealand type disclosure regime in Europe may meet resistance both from banks and national regulators. Indeed, such resistance can naturally be expected from both sides in a system prone to regulatory capture. So who should push for the implementation of a disclosure regime? Recent proposals from the Basle Committee on Banking Supervision on new international capital adequacy requirements explicitly mention market discipline and disclosure as a 'third pillar' of the new framework. These proposals are weak and non-committal, however. The Commission could possibly take the lead, proposing a new EU banking directive, but – judging from other attempts of banking legislation at the EU level – this process may be slow and uncertain.

There are several good reasons for the ECB to take action. The ECB is the only institution that naturally takes a European perspective on supervision. It has a general mandate to act under Article 105(6) of the Treaty. Moreover, according to Article 34 of the ESCB Statute, it can issue regulations in certain areas that become legally binding and directly applicable in all member states. The ECB has in fact already issued a regulation requiring financial institutions (banks, credit market institutions and money market funds) to produce monthly reports on their balance sheets. The main purpose of this regulation is to obtain statistics to follow the monetary developments in the euro area. But prudential supervision (treated under Article 25 (2)) is also cited as one of the tasks for which the ECB can issue such regulations. The ECB could not only mandate the financial institutions to extend their monthly reports to include the kind of information discussed above, but also to disclose it. For instance, the ECB could make public disclosure statements a requirement for using TARGET, or for being a counterparty to its repo operations. Even though these activities rest upon collateralised transactions, they are intimately connected with the interbank market, the most important source of systemic risk.

Reduce interbank exposure

A second aspect of reform should be to reduce the amount of uncollateralised interbank exposures among European banks. Interbank exposures carry the greatest risk of contagion and banks are not properly internalizing these externalities. There is thus a good case for intervention. Market-oriented reform could work via either pricing, increasing the cost of banks that expose the system to risk, or stimulating risk-reducing systems in markets and activities where they do not exist. Reforms should emphasise the following aims:

1. Diminish counterparty risk in payments and trading. TARGET, the existing centralised system for payments in euros, has limited contagion risks by shortening the lags in intra-European payments and by requiring collateral for

intra-day credits. But this is not enough: large foreign currency settlement risks could be limited by use of clearing houses and OTC markets for derivatives entail large counterparty risks that could be diminished by appropriate netting arrangements. The ECB could take the lead by insisting that such market arrangements be built in markets for euro-denominated assets. As in every aspect of the construction of Europe, the legal dimension may be an important drawback.

2. Stimulate banks to use collateralised markets to a greater degree. The repo market is much safer than the deposit market, even though both markets are used concurrently for the short-run supply of liquidity. This is bound to represent a market inefficiency seriously affecting systemic risk taking. True, interest rates on the repo market are lower than in the uncollateralised deposit market, but the wedge is likely to be insufficient. Indeed, when dealing in uncollaterised loans, individual financial institutions correctly price the counterparty risk but fail to internalize the systemic risk. The appropriate response is to allow the emergence of a single, safe interbank security market. As discussed in Chapter 1, the repo market is hampered by the limited use of cross-border collateral. Settlements systems for national security markets remain far from integrated; for example, there now exist 31 depositories in Europe, compared with just three in the US. Once again, national protectionist sentiment prevents this integration process from taking place and, in so doing, injects a dangerous dose of mispricing of systemic risk at the heart of the supply of liquidity. The ECB, which is responsible for systemic risk, has every reason to take the lead in promoting technically feasible, easy-to-take measures.

3. Stimulate banks to internalize systemic risk to a greater degree. The capital adequacy requirements can provide a natural incentive but current BIS proposals for new Basle rules offer little progress in that respect. The ECB is in an excellent position to take the initiative, not by acting alone but by using its legal right to make recommendations initiating Community legislation within its areas of competence. In the short run it can enhance transparency and, therefore, awareness of risks by reporting exposures in the interbank market. In the longer run, in cooperation with the BIS, it can set a maximum level of interbank market exposure to another bank – or to a bank holding company – as a proportion of the bank capital.

Prompt corrective action

Some financial institutions will eventually fail despite precautionary measures. How can the costs to society be limited? Avoiding a spill-over on other institutions creates a moral hazard – bailing out instead of liquidating failing institutions has been pervasive in continental Europe. What is needed is a mechanism that allows for the quick and orderly closure of a failing financial institution, possibly its acquisition by other institutions.

Foreign procedures indicate the way to go. New Zealand has an interesting mechanism in place, as described in Box 3.5 (pages 59–60). As part of the Federal Deposit Insurance Corporation Improvement Act (FDICIA), the US has adopted rules for *prompt corrective action* described in Box 3.6. Developing a similar bankruptcy code in Europe would not be very difficult since banks are already subject to capital regulation. It is essential to recognise that bankruptcy should only be the final move in a continuous process of transferring control from management to regulators. This enhances financial stability because it provides financial institutions with the guarantee of a smooth landing and pre-empts temptations for managers to gamble for resurrection.

Different regulatory regimes would imply that financial institutions in some countries face a lower regulatory cost. This is why harmonized regulation on this issue is critical. Pending EU legislation, it could be quickly achieved by adjusting and adopting a draft Directive on liquidation and reorganization of credit institutions that has been delayed for several years. As emphasised by Padoa-Schioppa (1999, p.7), we need a new directive 'to bring

---

BOX 3.6   Prompt corrective action in the US: the FDICIA

The US Saving and Loan crisis has shown how an ambiguous regulatory regime may jeopardise the financial sector soundness. To prevent future regulatory forbearance, the Federal Deposit Insurance Corporate Improvement Act of 1991 (FDICIA) mandates regulators to take prompt corrective action. The management of a financial institution can be partially dictated by the regulator even if the bank is solvent. Financial institutions are classified in five groups according to the risk of bankruptcy: well-capitalised, adequately capitalised, undercapitalised, significantly undercapitalised and critically undercapitalised. For each of the three last groups, there are requirements on the actions the managers have to perform. Thus, when a group falls into the undercapitalised class it is subjected to increase monitoring, it faces restrictions on the payment of dividend and management fees, on asset growth, on branching, on the issue of brokerage deposits, on the access to discount windows and must also implement an acceptable capital plan. If the situation deteriorates, additional restrictions will follow. The closing down of a financial institution in distress is automatic and, to minimise the risk of contagion, it is triggered when book value equity declines below 2% of assets, i.e. before the capital turns negative. In addition, insured depositors at failed institutions have access to their funds the next business day, through an advance from the Federal Deposit Insurance Corporation (FDIC). This limits the effect of the freezing of assets on economic transactions and economic activity (Benston and Kaufman, 1998). Interestingly, in order to make the cost of a bank rescue more transparent for taxpayers, a FDICIA regulation explicitly prohibits the FDIC from protecting uninsured depositors, except when there is systemic risk involved.

legal certainty to the framework of banking crisis management'. The ECB again has the possibility of contributing to more ambitious EU legislation through its ability to issue opinions and its ability to issue recommendations initiating new legislation.

3.5 | Conclusion: when to reform?

Much effort has gone into building a central bank that delivers high quality monetary policy. Much less attention has been paid to systemic risk and the costs of bank failures. This omission may partly reflect an understandable priority: monetary policy had to be operational as of 4 January 1999, while it was unlikely that a bank crisis would occur on that day, in the next month, or even in the following year. It may partly reflect an emphasis on building up ECB's credibility by adopting the Bundesbank as a role model; the Bundesbank is not in charge of regulation and supervision in Germany. It is certainly a consequence of Europe's difficulty in building centralised institutions when it entails shifting some prerogatives from the national to the Union level.

Fortunately, no financial crisis has occurred during the first year. Someday, it will. Is a major financial crisis needed to get the process of reform started in Europe? As noted by Kaufman (1999), in the US 'it took the severe banking and thrift crisis in the United States in the 1980s to enact the reform FDICIA legislation that reduced the discretionary power of the regulators'. It is obvious that waiting for a disaster to happen is not the best way to approach difficult political trade-offs. Recognizing these difficulties, we argue for a two-step strategy. We thus distinguish the first-best but politically involved, long-run solution from precautionary measures that can be enacted fairly quickly at the initiative of the ECB, whose Statutes unambiguously state its responsibility toward financial stability.

In the longer run, a centralised regulatory body will be essential to the smooth operation of European financial markets. It will undoubtedly be created one day, but that day is far off, and we simply cannot wait and hope for the best. Meanwhile some other solution must urgently be put in place. Relying on market discipline to buttress bank incentives in their approach to systemic risk does not require new institutions or transfers of power. What is needed is to increase transparency through disclosure rules that function elsewhere, to decrease the risk of contagion by stimulating safer exposures in the interbank market and to adopt harmonised country-level procedures for prompt corrective action and orderly closure in case of financial institution failure. The reforms that we propose would help meet the challenges of preserving financial stability in the wake of closer financial integration in the euro area. We haven't seen any better alternative.

To summarise, the ECB has succeeded in the areas in which it is directly in control: monetary policy and a large value real-time payment system. In the areas where the ECB has only general responsibility (efficiency and stability of the financial environment, regarding cross-border retail payment systems, cross-border mergers) not much has been done. The view that ECB has no authority on financial competition is excessively formal. The ECB can and should take leadership in this area and promote the adoption of adequate financial legislation.

4

Conclusions and proposals

Background

It will take years – possibly decades – for Europe to shape its own brand of central banking. In its first year and under intense scrutiny the ECB has taken only a few steps in this direction. Unsurprisingly, Europe's deep ambivalence towards integration is already surfacing and affecting the working of the Eurosystem. European federalists wish to see the ECB in the driver's seat along with a centralised body in charge of banking supervision and regulation. Supporters of a Europe of Nations, on the other hand, are reluctant to centralise more than a bare minimum authority. This scene is familiar from other areas of economic integration and shows up also in the ambiguous positions of the European Commission and the European Parliament.

This common ambivalence is keenly felt in the area of central banking because the creation of a single currency is fundamentally a step towards centralisation. From the pure perspective of economic efficiency, it makes little sense to keep national central banks and banking regulators in place and it is fairly clear in which direction the winds of history are blowing. Moving too fast, though, is neither advisable nor politically feasible. Detours and backlashes must be accepted as the price to pay for a unique experiment decided upon in Maastricht nearly a decade ago. The rocky road might once have appeared as a good enough reason to cancel the trip, but – once underway – the task is to find feasible solutions that minimise the risks of serious difficulties.

The ECB faces these challenges at a time when the approach to central banking is in a flux. In monetary policy ideas continuously develop, reflecting the prevailing economic conditions and advances in our understanding. The results of a period with anti-inflationary policies along with a return to sustained growth, possibly fuelled by a discrete technological advance – the so-called IT revolution – have made the objectives of monetary policy more ambitious, as reflected in narrower and more precise inflation targets in many countries. Heightened sensitivity to credibility requires that central banks send increasingly precise signals. Deepening globalization of financial markets, creating a denser web of interbank linkages and enhancing the force of market reactions, raises the stakes in maintaining financial stability. Growing recognition of the needs for democratic control over economic policy-making brings to the fore demands for accountability, which are particularly exacting in Euroland where public opinions remain further apart than in a single nation state.

Our report not only takes account of these constraints, but put them at the centre of this year's analysis. It recognises the unique situation of the ECB and attempts to map out some of the problems ahead. The report highlights two issues of monetary and financial stability where Europe's ambivalence towards its own future matters most: how should the ECB communicate its analyses and decisions, and what approach should be taken in banking regulation and supervision. Our detailed proposals are developed in Chapters 2 and 3 and recalled in the Executive Summary. In this chapter, we spell out the measures the Eurosystem itself can undertake fairly quickly and easily, and those that require Treaty revisions.

4.2 Measures that can be adopted in 2000

Retail transfers   Ordinary citizens have watched with awe the arrival of EMU, but so far they little has affected their daily lives. Those well informed may understand that we are indeed in a new world with a single central bank controlling a single currency, but a situation with much excitement and few tangible achievements can easily backfire. Since little can be done to hasten the day when euros will circulate, the least that can be done is to make cross-border payments within Euroland as easy and cheap as within a member country. Wholesale transfers are easy and cheap, thanks to TARGET and other systems. Bringing down the costs of retail transfers facilitating cross-border banking is clearly in the realm of the possible. The ECB and bank supervisors can quickly agree to push hard on banks to leave antiquated and anti-competitive practices – such as correspondent banking – to make this happen.

Liquidity provision   Current ECB auction procedures combine a fixed interest rate with rationing. This mechanism entails huge and variable allotment ratios, a source of inefficiency as the fixed rate does not reflect the true cost borne by banks to acquire liquidity.

While part of the Bundesbank tradition, the procedure of fixed rate/fixed quantity auctions does not relate in any meaningful way to the ECB's credibility and ability to enforce price stability. Reforming the procedure in favour of market clearing is an entirely technical issue that does not involve any deep issue of centralisation vs. national prerogatives. By not taking such a simple step, the ECB unnecessarily exposes itself to the criticism of setting principles of continuity ahead of market efficiency.

The ECB's Communication Strategy   Creative ambiguity may be useful in a few instances. But it must be traded off against the uncertainty that it creates, which ultimately translates into higher and more volatile borrowing costs. For a variety of reasons, including the need to build up a common approach within its Governing Council, the ECB has so far erred on the side of ambiguity. Both theory and recent practice suggest that *ex ante* transparency is a superior regime. The ECB can freely decide to release its own forecasts for Euroland inflation (and output) and explain its policy decisions as the choice among alternative contingency plans tied to the forecast distributions.

Long-term bond rates povide one illustration of the problem. The surprisingly strong influence of US conditions on European interest rates appears to reflect the markets' belief that the euro will not be left to fluctuate much vs. the dollar. While too wide exchange rate movements are clearly undesirable, too much dependence on US monetary conditions is unhealthy. But this trade-off ought to be a matter of choice for the ECB, not automatically imposed by market expectations. A decoupling of European long-term rates requires precisely less ambiguity in the ECB's communication about policy.

A shift towards *ex ante* transparency about the policy strategy would go deeper into inherited traditions. Ambiguity is a way of keeping close to the chest cards that may occasionally be useful, but it carries a cost in terms of imprecise and potentially misleading statements that must be amended under pressure. It also allows papering over of internal divergences, but then may lead observers to imagine more than is actually true. What worked well for the Bundesbank – in different times and circumstances – and other central banks steeped in the same tradition is not the right approach for the ECB.

As long as the ECB lives under the present rules of the Treaty, we do not agree with the critics who argue for a breach of the current collective accountability of the Council by releasing individual voting records and minutes with attribution of individual divergences of opinion.

Banking regulation and supervision   Euroland bank supervision and regulation is currently in the hands of national authorities, sometimes inside, sometimes outside the central bank, with considerable harmonization within the framework of the Basle accord. Supervisory and regulatory information is thus mostly at the national level. Banks so far remain largely national, but the situation is likely to change quickly. Yet, emergency intervention to deal with large enough institutions or with systemic threats to financial stability has to be conducted at the Euroland level. Interbank linkages and other cross-border market interactions among banks may already make it impossible for individual national supervisors to handle emergencies on their own. In the present regime, however, financial crisis management has to rely on improvised coordination.

The most appropriate response – centralisation – seems beyond reach, at present. But that does not mean that the best course of action is to wait and see whether the present system is, as we believe, inadequate. Several steps can be taken quickly in the direction of a complementary set of decentralised measures. One is to require a New Zealand-style approach of full public disclosure of harmonized bank accounts. This would enhance information to everyone about the health of individual institutions and promote market-based monitoring of bank practices. A second step is to promote safer interbank transactions and thus reduce the dangers of contagion among European banks in the event of financial failures. This should involve the immediate removal of existing market barriers, as those that keep the collateralised repo market from growing at the expense of the uncollateralised deposit market and – in the slightly longer run – reformed capital requirements, giving banks better incentives to internalize the systemic risk they impose on others. A third step is to require European-wide rules of US-style prompt corrective action and orderly closure of failing banks.

These steps should ideally be implemented by new European Banking Directives, including (a beefed up version of) the stalled Directive on liquidation and re-organization measures for credit institutions. The ECB should use its constitutional right to issue recommendations initiating such European legislation. In some cases the ECB could use its own constitutional right to issue binding regulations for the Euroland countries.

4.3 Measures that require Treaty revisions

The Maastricht and Amsterdam Treaties constitute a veritable *tour de force*. They have made the transition to monetary union and its first year of existence as uneventful as anyone could have dreamt. But they are not the last word. Indeed, a new Inter-Governmental Conference (IGC) is scheduled to start in 2000 with the specific task of preparing the EU for the accession of between five and ten new member states. This is an opportunity to undertake a number of Treaty revisions. Given Europe's ambivalence noted at the outset of this chapter, we do not expect all of our proposals to be adopted. Putting them on the agenda will hasten the day when they are.

Representation By its design the Governing Council of the ECB represents national interests. This is a potential source of unhelpful disagreements over policy, and appointment decisions coloured by national politics. The design also misses the fact that European monetary policy decisions affect groups in society that cut across national borders. Better representation of European interests could be achieved by reducing the dominating presence of NCB governors and giving the European Parliament a greater say in appointing ECB Board members drawn from a wider pool than professional central bankers.

Policy-making would still be set by the ECB Council but its size – already uncomfortably large and bound to grow even further as EMU membership expands – would be limited to a set number. For example, the Council would consist of, say, eleven members, six of whom would constitute the Executive Board (reduced by one member), and the five other voting members would be NCB governors rotating according to a pre-set schedule. Their respective governments would still appoint NCB governors, while the ECB Board members could be chosen by the European Parliament. This procedure would enhance both the competence and representation of Board members.

The latter aspect would be better served by a European Parliament elected along different lines than today with a stronger role for pan-European parties. An example – beyond the scope of this report – would be to elect half the members via party lists on a proportional Europe-wide system, and the other half via single-member districts. This would increase the Parliament's representativness and accountability, and stimulate campaigns where pan-European issues figure prominently in contrast to the current system where elections reflect mostly domestic issues.

Accountability Accountability will still be limited, however, as long as the Eurosystem exercises political responsibilities by being goal-independent. The task of defining the goals of monetary policy – mainly to set a precise inflation target – should be given to a politically accountable, i.e. an elected body. Then, and only then, could an instrument-independent ECB focus on the technical task of fulfilling these goals, as befit a non-elected institution. Such reform would contribute to fewer national tensions in policy-making and to less contentious appointments. Votes and views of individual Council members would then be much less sensitive material than today.

The task of determining the goal could be attributed to the ECOFIN Council, subject to approval by the European Parliament, or directly to the Parliament (after appropriate electoral reform). The goal could be set at regular, say three-year intervals (reasonably long periods are needed given the lags in monetary policy). An over-ride clause could provide for unscheduled changes in the target as a response to exceptional events. The clause could be activated at the request of ECOFIN or the European Parliament. The ECB would naturally report to its political principal(s) on the progress towards meeting the goal and would be formally required to explain any substantial departures.

Regulation and supervision   The logic of a single currency implies the emergence of transnational banks which, in turn, implies centralised regulation and supervision. This transfer of responsibility requires changes in European legislation, which go beyond the current practice of Commission directives carried out by national bodies. Such a move involves no particular technical difficulty but three issues arise. First, is the transfer of authority, which is politically contentious. Second, is the decision of whether or not regulation and supervision should be exercised by the ECB or an independent body. The trend is to set up independent bodies to avoid conflict of interest within the central bank. If this trend is followed and an independent body is set up, there will be the need to decide how to appoint its officers and where to locate it. Third, is how to pay for crisis interventions decided by the new body. Here one could imagine different sharing rules. More important than the precise choice would be that some binding rule is really firmly in place, such that swift action – in the exceptional cases when it is really needed – is not stifled by national haggling over how to split the cost.

References

Akerlof, G., W. Dickens, and G. Perry (1996) 'The Macroeconomics of Low Inflation, *Brookings Papers on Economic Activity*, 1, 1–76.

Begg, D. et al. (1998) *The ECB: Safe at Any Speed?*, Monitoring the European Central Bank 1, CEPR.

Benston, G. and G. Kaufman, (1998) 'Deposit Insurance Reform in the FDIC Improvement Act: the experience to date' *Economic Perspectives* (Federal Reserve Bank of Chicago) Second Quarter 1998, pp. 2–20.

Bernanke, B., T. Laubach, F. Mishkin, and A. Posen (1999) *Inflation Targeting: Lessons from the International Experience*, Princeton University Press.

Brimmer, A. F. (1989), 'Central Banking and Systemic Risks in Capital Markets' Distinguished Lecture on Economics in Government, *Journal of Economic Perspectives*, 3, pp. 3-16.

Buiter, W. (1999a) 'Alice in Euroland', CEPR Policy Paper No. 1, CEPR

Buiter, W. (1999b) 'Monetary Misperceptions', Mimeo, Bank of England.

Calomiris, C. (1999) 'The IMF's Imprudent Role as Lender of Last Resort', *The Cato Journal*, Vol. 17, N°3.

Clarida, R., J. Gali and M.Gertler (1998) 'Monetary Policy Rules in Practice', *European Economic Review*, 42, pp. 1033–68.

Clarida, R. and M. Gertler (1997) 'How Does the Bundesbank Conduct Monetary Policy' in Romer, C. and D. Romer (eds), *Reducing Inflation: Motivation and Strategy*, University of Chicago Press.

Coenen, G. and J-L. Vega (1999) 'The Demand for M3 in the Euro Area', ECB Working Paper No. 6.

Cordella T. and E.. L. Yeyati (1998) 'Public Disclosure and Bank Failures' *International Monetary Fund Staff Papers*, 45(1), pp. 110–31.

Danthine, J. P., F. Giavazzi, X.Vives and E.. L. von Thadden, (1999) *The Future of European Banking*, Monitoring European Integration 9, CEPR.

Danthine, J. P., F. Giavazzi and E.. L.von Thadden (1999) 'The Effect of EMU on Financial Markets: A First Assessment', Mimeo, DEEP, Université de Lausanne.

De Bandt, O. and P. Hartmann, (1998) 'What is Systemic Risk Today?' Mimeo, European Central Bank,

Dewatripont, M. et al (1995) *Flexible Intergration: Towards a More Effective and Democratic Europe*, Monitoring European Integration 6, CEPR.

Di Noia C. and G. Di Giorgio (1999) 'Should Banking Supervision and Monetary Policy Tasks Be Given to Different Agencies'? Mimeo, Università La Sapienza, Rome.

Eichengreen, B. and C. Wyplosz (1993) 'Unstable EMS', *Brookings Papers on Economic Activity*, 1, 1993.

Eijffinger, S. and J. de Haan (1996) The Political Economy of Central Bank Independence, Special Paper in International Economics No. 19, Princeton University.

Fatas, A. (1998) 'Does EMU Need a Fiscal Federation?', *Economic Policy* 26, pp. 163–204, Blackwell Publishers.

Faust, J. (1996) 'Whom Can We Trust to Run the Fed? Theoretical Support for the Founders' Views', *Journal of Monetary Economics,* 37, pp. 267–83.

Faust, J. and L. E. O. Svensson (1999) 'Transparency and Credibility: Monetary Policy with Unobservable Goals', Mimeo, IIES.

Fischer, S. (1995) 'The Unending Search for Monetary Salvation', *NBER Macroeconomics Annual 1995*, MIT Press.

Furfine, C. (1999) 'Internbank Exposures: Quantifying the Risk of Contagion', BIS Working paper, No. 70.

Geerats, P. (1999) 'Transparency and Reputation: Should the ECB Publish Its Inflation Forecasts?', Working Paper, UC Berkeley.

Goodfriend, M. (1993) 'Interest Rate Policy and the Inflation Scare Problem', *Federal Reserve Bank of Richmond Economic Quarterly, 79*, pp. 1–24.

Goodhart, C. and D. Schoenmaker (1995) 'Should the Functions of Monetary Policy and Banking Supervision Be Separated?' *Oxford Economic Papers, 47*(4), pp. 539–60.

Gorton, G, (1988) 'Banking Panics and Business Cycles' *Oxford Economic Papers, 40*(4), pp. 751–81.

Grilli, V., D. Masciandaro, and G. Tabellini (1991) 'Political and Monetary Institutions and Public Financial Policies in the Industrial Countries', *Economic Policy*, 13, pp. 341–92, Blackwell Publishers.

IMF (1999) 'Progress with European Monetary Intergration'.

Issing, O. (1999) 'The Eurosystem: Transparent and Accountable, or Willem in Euroland', CEPR Policy Paper, No. 2, CEPR

Kaufman, G. (1999) 'Banking and Currency Crises and Systemic Risk: A Taxonomy and Review', Mimeo, Loyola University Chicago and Federal Reserve Bank of Chicago

King, M. (1997) 'The Inflation Target Five Years On', Lecture given at the LSE, Mimeo, Bank of England.

Kreps, D. (1990) 'Corporate Culture and Economic Theory' in Alt, J. and K.Shepsle (eds), *Perspectives on Positive Political Economy*, Cambridge University Press.

Laffont, J-J. and D. Martimort (1998) 'Transaction Costs, Institutional Design and the Separation of Powers' *European Economic Review, 42*(3-5), pp. 673–84

Lannoo, K. 'Financial Supervision in EMU', Center for European Policy Studies Working Paper, 1999

McCauley, R. and W. White (1997) 'The Euro and European Financial Markets', BIS Working Paper, No. 41.

Padoa-Schioppa, T. (1999) 'EMU and Banking Supervision' London School of Economics lecture.

Persson, T. and G. Tabellini (2000) *Political Economics: Explaining Economic Policy*, MIT Press, forthcoming.

Piketty, T. (1999) 'The Information-Aggregation Approach to Political Institutions', *European Economic Review*, 43, pp. 791–800.

Santomero, A. and Hoffman, 1998, 'Problem Bank Resolution: Evaluating the Options', Financial Institutions Center W.P. pp. 98–105

Svensson, L. (1999) 'Monetary Policy Issues for the Eurosystem, Carnegie-Rochester Conference Series, forthcoming.

Tabellini, G. (1999) ' The Monthly Bulletins of the European Central Bank: A Comment'.

Tirole, J. (1996) 'A Theory of Collective Reputations (with Applications to the Persistence of Corruption and Firm Quality)', *Review of Economic Studies*, 63, pp. 1–22.

Sibert, A. (1999) 'Monetary Policy Committees: Individual and Collective Reputations', Mimeo, Birkbeck College.

von Hagen, J. (1995) 'Inflation and Monetary Targeting in Germany' in Leiderman, L. and L.E.O. Svensson (eds), *Inflation Targets*, CEPR.

White, W. R. (1998) 'The Coming Transformation of Continental European Banking?' Bank for International Settlements Working Paper Series, 54.